In the Company
of Trout

We hope you'll enjoy
This light hearted
look at your Fly Fishing
Roots

Mom & Dad
1999

In the Company of Trout

True Stories, Ruminations, and Vermont Guidance

Peter Shea

The New England Press, Inc.
Shelburne, Vermont

Cover illustration from the original watercolor
"Upper Lamoille River" by Robert Popick

Photographs pp. 19, 38, 55, 76, 91 by Ron Clark

First Edition
Printed in the United States of America

Library of Congress Catalog Card Number: 99-066812
ISBN 1-881535-34-7

For additional copies of this book or for a catalog of our
other New England titles, please write:

The New England Press
P.O. Box 575
Shelburne, VT 05482

or e-mail: nep@together.net

Visit us on the Web at www.nepress.com

Contents

Introduction 1

Fishing Lies 3

A More Careful Reading of Thoreau 7

The Upper Connecticut River 11

Leadeth Me Beside Still Waters 21

Secrets to Big Brookies (and Lakers too) 28

The Averill Lakes 31

The Key to Paradise 39

A Creature of the Night 47

Little Rock Pond 53

Things That Go Bump in the Water 57

Ducking at Duck 61

Holland Pond and Neighbors 69

My Fishing Rods 77

Getting Chummy 82

The Oh-What-the-Hell Cast 85

The Lamoille River 88

Short Lines 93

The Last Cast 101

Introduction

One: If you are like me, this is the only "introduction" to a fishing book that you will ever read, and you did so because you could see that it was three sentences long. Two: All the stories told here are absolutely true. Three: In that great tradition of angling reports, this absolute truth is especially true when it comes to the size of the fish.

Fishing Lies

In the end, stream fishing for trout is a solitary sport, so I forgive my father that it wasn't until I was eight years old that he took me along for the first time. Now that he is gone, I realize that "trout fishing" and a love of all things outdoors have been his potent legacy to me.

My going fishing was certainly a rite of passage. Before I went along, I can recall his Saturday comings-and-goings. I recall his smell—sweat, cigarettes, and beer—mingling on his hands and canvas jacket with the smell of freshly caught brookies.

At his return, we would fill the large enamel sink with water. His eyes came alive with mischief. One by one, he would extract the dressed fish from his game pockets and rinse off the bits of dirt and fern that clung to them. My eyes would widen when he held one or two of them upright in the sink and feigned their swimming. And I would laugh wildly on the cusp of panic and ecstasy when he swerved one, barracuda-like, at my tentatively outstretched fingers. *Gotcha!*

Where did those exotic creatures come from? What was their world like? How could you catch them?

At length all those answers, and more, came from him. I recall a fateful Friday night that I stayed up until ten o'clock in preparation for the next day's baptism. We were tying six-foot leaders onto #6 and #8 hooks, and I vividly remember his three great instructions:

> *If you see someone fishing the brook, give him a fair stretch of water before you set in to fish.*
>
> *If you make a fish bleed, you must keep it.*
>
> *Never, ever, EVER break a fish n' game law.*

Sixteen trout seasons had come and gone since that first trout fishing trip. It was 1971.

It was a spectacular October afternoon. I was fishing a picture-postcard tributary of the Connecticut River. The forest's leaves were aflame with color. The sky was such a rare deep blue that it didn't belong in Vermont. It had gotten lost somewhere over Wyoming and was stopping here only for the day before it would resume its search for a home over the Atlantic Ocean.

I had spent the last year in a hot and foreign land, where I had daily fantasies about returning to Vermont, to be among friends, to be free of dysentery. For many months I had dreamt about trout fishing again, and this fishing excursion was, in my mind, a metaphor for my reintroduction to the real world. I had arrived in northern Vermont in the thrill of early October's colors and spawn, and I was back where I belonged.

But when the uniformed gentleman tapped me on the shoulder, I was nearly turning blue from holding in a grand lung-full of some of the finest marijuana ever to surface in the Green Mountain State. I had just sucked it in from a generously rolled joint and I was about to return it to my fishing buddy. The officer had materialized without sight or sound. *Gotcha!*

Oh my god, I thought, the State Police. I am busted.

Then, in less than two seconds, I did the following: crushed out the illicit roach in my bare palm (*youch!*), bent over at precisely 180 degrees from the officer, stretched my neck to maximum extension, and tried to set the world speed and distance record for exhaling marijuana smoke.

If my compadre hadn't been equally freaked out, he would have busted a gut laughing at my worthy-of-a-dervish body movements. And what did the man in the uniform think I was doing with these bizarre body contortions? I get embarrassed just imagining it. As to his perception . . . well, I have no certain knowledge. He was, however, a fish and game warden, not a state trooper.

To this day I don't really know if my impulsive, smoke-blowing gyration tactics succeeded or not. Perhaps the warden was completely naive and thought I was overcome by fear and was about to hurl lunch on the stream bank. If by any chance he was "enlightened," I'm sure it was all he could do to keep a straight face at my antics. Regardless, he totally ignored the joint and went about his business—the fish and game laws.

When it became apparent that the officer was only interested in our angling activities a tide of relief rolled over me. That feeling was only short lived, however. After all, I was getting busted for something far more important than blowing some weed. I was being arrested for a violation of the FISH AND GAME LAWS.

I was mortified beyond words and began running a horrible variety of mental movies to myself of my father discovering my loathsome transgression. What would he think of me?!

"Let me see your fishing licenses, fellahs. Did you know that this is trout water? Did you know that trout season closed about three weeks ago?" The questions came in rapid succession, without pause for answer. As he asked them, I let the roach drop to my feet and surreptitiously ground it to dust under the heel of my boot.

Of course, we knew full well that for the rest of the world, trout fishing was over until next spring. It was a mere quirk of fate that had returned me to Vermont a couple of weeks after trout season had ended. And as to licenses . . . well, if you're going to fish out of season, what's the point of having a fishing license? Such had been the twisted thought processes governing this breach of conduct.

To the warden, I said nothing.

He wrote the summons, confiscated our rods and all the tackle, and bid us good-bye.

We sat down with knees shaking. We laughed and joked about our brush with what could have been the deep legal waters of drug offenses. I showed my co-conspirator the hand wound I had gained in crushing out the roach. Although I didn't speak of it as such, I took it to be a stigmata of my fish-and-game sin. It was my very own scarlet letter. Its physical impression blistered and lingered for months. Its psychic impression haunts me yet.

A couple of weeks later we went before the judge, who in his wisdom fined us fifty dollars each and yanked our privilege to fish for a whole year. By way of a taunt, our rods and tackle were returned. There is not the least doubt that I would have gladly done a couple of off-season months on Devil's Island in return for the sanction of fishing that following summer. It was not to be. Instead I found myself dreaming about trout fishing for yet another year. Dreaming about fishing . . . and *lying*. Lying to my father, the man who had planted within me the strange and exquisite yearning to fish—a wondrous gift and one of the ways he still lives on within me.

The spring and summer of 1972 were tough for trout fishing. I made that clear to my father when we talked on the phone every couple weeks. We had very few seasons left to fish together, although I didn't know it at the time.

Water's been too cold, Dad . . . Water's been too high . . . Been too busy with work, Dad . . . Car's been broke . . . Got a new girlfriend . . . Water's been too low . . . Gonna try to get out next week, Dad . . . I'll get out for sure before the season closes.

A More Careful
Reading of Thoreau

One fine morning a friend from Winooski joined up with me to go fishing. We went out to catch big fish in the upper Connecticut River. We staked out a spot on the west side of the river at the breached dam at Lyman Falls, just a few miles upstream from Bloomfield. I sat on the remnants of the old concrete structure, attending the big hole downstream. My friend headed upstream a hundred yards or so and cast through an inviting run of water, slick and deep.

I am still not beyond using bait, now and again, and the stiff skunking I had received the day before using flies prompted me to go for a can of crawlers. My hopes were high. My friend, a dedicated spin fisherman, had brought along an impressive variety of hardware to meet the challenge.

As the morning progressed, that initial optimism began to fade, and our hopes for a record-breaker had been reduced to settling for even a single bite. We were having absolutely no luck.

As the noon hour approached, three fellows appeared on the New Hampshire side, baited up and, to use my friend's brashly graphic term, began "gangfishing" the deep run on the east side.

Although our poor luck persisted, that was not the case with the threesome on the gravel bar across the way. They were having a day for the record books. Every ten minutes or so, one of them would let loose with a cowboy-style scream, "YEE-HAW!" Fish on. The rest of the gang would start whooping and hollering, then jumping up and down with electric enthusiasm as one of their party held an arched rod high against the stiff current.

In short order, one of them would produce the net, and they all would gather together as the fish was landed and added to their stringer. With each addition, the stringer was re-staked to the shore with progressively larger sharpened sticks.

At first we took these goings-on to be an auspicious indication that our own angling fortunes were going to change. But as the hour passed our feelings of renewed hope gradually eroded. In its place grew that green fiend—jealousy. What the hell were those guys using? Worms? Crawlers? Were they on the bottom? How were they doing it? We craned our necks and strained our eyes for a clue but just couldn't discern any useful information.

Again and again the threesome yelped and squealed with delight, jumping like spit on a griddle, as one of their number would come on to a fish and land it. At length my friend and I were in near as much of a lather as the fellows on the other side. We were absolutely beside ourselves about how to improve our own situation.

Finally we concluded that the reason for their success was, like the old marketing maxim says, location, location, and location. And, well, courtesy and pride be damned, we were going to the other side and add two more to the group that was *gangfishing* this productive run.

We reeled in, headed for the car, the bridge at Bloomfield/ North Stratford, and (we thought) certain success on the New Hampshire side of the river.

My old Dodge Coronet station wagon was a real low rider and had been more than two months without a reverse gear. The farm road that went down and across the railroad tracks was a lousy bet for the short trip, so we parked in the pull-off alongside Route 3, right next to a brand new, long-model Land Rover with a Dartmouth Faculty Parking Permit on its rear door window. We surmised correctly that it belonged to the fishermen we had been observing. We were amused that they drove a Land Rover but wouldn't take it all the way down. We were also amused by the bumper sticker it sported: "American Lit Majors Satisfy Thoreau-ly."

We unloaded our gear as quickly as we could and made it posthaste toward the spot we knew was red hot.

"How's the luck?" we petitioned meekly on arrival.

"Great!" piped up one of them, who was echoed enthusiastically by the other two. "Yeah, terrific! Great! Just unbelievable—fabulous fishing!"

"Big ones?" we prodded further.

"You bet!" said one as he scooted over to the stake that held the stringer, reached down, and held up the catch.

We nearly choked as the fish were lifted from the water with a tumultuous flapping and flopping, like a Medusa's head. All three of them were beaming like the winners of a national derby as the catch was displayed. There, before our eyes, was the most impressive stringer—indeed, one would have to say the *only* stringer—of river chubs that we had ever seen.

At a complete loss for words, we bid a quick good-bye and headed up the hill. Once out of earshot, we just about collapsed laughing as we repeatedly reproduced that little guttural "quacking" sound that chubs are prone to make when you take the hook out of them. Of course we were laughing both at the naive fishermen and ourselves. For, let's face it, we were willing to pick up stakes, drive six or seven miles, and jump in on our neighbor's fishing hole for the sake of some unsavory chubs.

As to the successful college-bred anglers from Dartmouth? Well, they continued fishing for the chubs. They should have given their Thoreau a more *thorough* reading, however. He did not mince words when it came to chub meat. To quote the old Master of Walden Pond: "It tastes like brown paper salted."

Bon appetit.

The Upper Connecticut River

As consolation prizes go, I suppose the right to fish the Connecticut River with a Vermont fishing license is not such a bad one. Keeping this in mind has given me a grudging peace with a certain 1933 U.S. Supreme Court decision. It was then that the country's highest court, finally and forever, ceded Vermont's very best piece of moving trout water. New Hampshire claimed the prize.

With that Supreme Court decision, the Vermont-New Hampshire boundary line became the average low water mark on the Vermont side of the Connecticut River. What it has sugared down to, for us fishing folk, is not such a bad deal: they own the river (bridge maintenance and all), while a resident Vermont fishing license is a valid ticket to this sweet silver sliver of the Granite State. And, for those of us who are seeking maximum compensation for this untoward collision of history and geography, there is yet another prize. The Vermont fishing license also currently works on the New Hampshire tributaries of this river, right up to where their first highway bridge crosses the given tributary . . . a word to the wise and the vengeful.

11

The Connecticut River has a rich history and pre-history. The Abenaki planted corn on the fertile meadows of its flood-plains. It was, along with the Hudson and the St. Lawrence rivers, one of the main access routes to the interior of this part of the New World. Punctuated at first by a series of forts, early settlement in Vermont followed the river's stem northward, advancing and retreating as wars with our European cousins and the native peoples ebbed and flowed.

Long before the river saw the great log drives of the latter half of the nineteenth century, Atlantic salmon swam in its waters, ascending upstream at least as far as Beecher Falls. The earliest maps record its Native American name as "Kwini-teguh" or "Long River." It is a name well earned, for it is more than 400 miles long. And herein lies a little obstinate personal irony. In the more than forty years I have fished it, I have nearly always fished upstream of Bloomfield, in the first twenty-five-mile-long leg of its 200-mile Vermont visit. I have never felt in the least shortchanged. From "the Gore," where the river first touches Vermont, downstream to where the Nulhegan River enters it in Bloomfield is one of the finest pieces of fishing real estate that a Vermont license purchases.

Here, the flat narrow valley of the Connecticut, cradled between the mountains of both states, holds a river that can enchant anyone who fishes for trout. It is picturesque, it has plenty of volume, and it runs cold. In places, the river takes its leave of the road and meanders far enough away to dissuade all but the most dogged anglers. The result is that the river has miles of some of the most underfished trout water in the north-eastern United States.

It is not just the occasional appearance of a Yellowstone-style driftboat that now prompts its comparison to a Western river. The upper Connecticut River certainly bears resemblance to the classic Western river. It is big water, with its runs, riffles, and slicks measured in hundreds of yards. Walk to its banks in any of several spots and a full day's careful fishing is within this single view. It has holes deep enough to hold browns and rain-bows of uncanny size. There is nearly always a good flow, and although it doesn't run as cold as its true Western counterparts, it will generally run cooler than other northern Vermont rivers, such as the Lamoille, the Winooski, or the Missisquoi.

For starters, its impoundment and controlled release from Lake Francis (eighty-five feet deep) provides a cooling effect throughout the season's warmer days. This reach of the Connecticut is also about a thousand feet higher than the lower stems of those other Vermont rivers, where they begin to resemble the Connecticut in size and volume. This elevation difference alone would predict average air temperature differences of about four degrees. Thick forest cover and a watershed that rapidly plunges from 3,000-foot mountains also help keep the water cool. The result on the fishing is perceptible. While the lower reaches of the rivers entering the Champlain Valley can go dead during summer's dog days, it's only an extraordinary hot spell that will put a lid on the fishing in the Upper Connecticut. For much of the season the Connecticut will run at temperatures optimal for active trout, and even on the warmest days you can still expect to see at least some activity at dusk.

Unlike Western rivers, however, just about all of this part of the Connecticut is accessible to the public on foot as well as by driftboat. Vermonters have much to appreciate about river and stream access in the Green Mountain State. It is just about the opposite on "trouty" sections of the Yellowstone and the Madison. There, one can drive miles to find the next public fishing access, while large sections of these rivers are off limits to bank fishing and, at least for practical purposes, wading as well. On the upper Connecticut River, you drive miles to find a posting, and most of the river remains accessible to the angler.

The lack of fishing pressure here has made it comfortable for most of the landowners to have a pretty easygoing attitude about letting you get to the river. When in doubt, though, one should always ask. Continued access to the river is dependent on the ongoing good behavior of anglers that can justify the landowners' generosity.

The Vermont side of the river offers easier access. Vermont 102 is a much quieter highway than U.S. Route 3. Between

Bloomfield and Lemington there are around a dozen well established pull-offs and scores of other opportunities.

On the New Hampshire side of the river, there are a couple of developed public accesses. These are on the trophy stretch of water that runs between Bloomfield, Vermont, and North Stratford, New Hampshire. This is textbook trout water to which anyone chasing trout owes a visit. It a piece of water that illustrates why the establishment of no-kill zones is such a good idea. Fishing is restricted to the use of artificial lures or flies only. The no-kill regulation requires all fish to be immediately released back to the water, unharmed. This kind of protection has paid off big time, as the area holds good numbers of discerning browns and rainbows (especially browns). These have gained wisdom as well as pounds over the years.

Except in the case of an obvious hatch, there is no question that spin fishing will produce better results than casting a fly, if for no other reason than you can cover more water and go deeper. (See "ugly" below for the exception.) Spring will see long, wide runs of broken whitewater. Within these areas the water presents myriad holding pockets and short, fast-moving slicks. Nearly all of these hold trout.

Spring wading should be approached with abundant caution. The river has quite a push to it here. A steep enough grade will endow knee-high water with the ability to literally sweep you off your feet. In this reach, there is frequently a good side and a bad side to the river. The good side has relatively small cobbles or coarse hardpan gravel and grades slowly deeper as you move toward its center. The bad side has a bottom consisting of an irregular distribution of slippery boulders. (There may be a tenuous foothold of gravel scattered here and there among them.) The underfoot rocks can range in size from cantaloupes to small household furniture, and they make for a challenging walk. For staying high and dry, felt-soled boots are your best bet. A wading staff would also be a plus. (So why don't I own one?) Even with the best precautions it is easy to get lured into some rather hairy spots. Recognize that there're plenty of places where those who

14

throw the fly were never meant to reach. Except, maybe, by boat!

In recent years, guided float trips have made their appearance. It is a great way to reach some water that, otherwise, never gets fished with a fly. Whether by boat or on foot, anyone who is not content unless they have cast their fly over every pocket and run will find frustration here. There is just too much water to cover.

Right below Lyman Falls Dam, just upstream of the no-kill zone, is a spot popular with locals from both sides of the river. The dam was breached many years ago, and its remnants are still visible on either side of the river. There are deep holes on both sides that annually give up huge fish.

Other hot spots for me have been below the Columbia Bridge, the "Hospital Run" in Colebrook, and the entry points for several tributaries. The water either side of where Simms Stream enters has been a personal haunt since childhood, but the character of the water is not the classic fast moving, rocky bottom that one usually associates with trouty water. Willard Stream is another great spot; it will see some spawning rainbows in the spring.

Some of my very favorite runs of the river are upstream of Beecher Falls, in the Gore. "The Gore" is that unique piece of Vermont real estate from which you travel to New Hampshire by going north *or* south. For me, one of the fascinations of this part of the river is its sneak brook trout population. I say "sneak" because generally in Vermont, once one of our rivers runs downstream far enough to gain any size, the brook trout fishing is generally shot. This water is exceptional. Although the trophy quarry remains browns and rainbows, in that order, the brook trout here are notable. The first time I fished it, I was shocked by taking ten- to twelve-inch brookies on an indiscriminate succession of streamer flies.

When the water is up a little but still running clear, the rowdy stretches of the river are my favorite places to pull a great flyfishing trick out of my bag. It is a technique that was taught to me by a fishing partner of thirty years who has been holed up in Montana for about half that time. He calls the technique "fishin' ugly." I call it "hard-hat nymphing" or "the near-bait experience."

Fishing ugly gets its name from how it looks. It is ungainly, inelegant, lazy, and nearly haphazard—not to mention a little dangerous. It is a kind of fishing that you elect under two conditions. One, nothing else is working, or two, you are determined to catch *big* fish.

I became a convert during an entire morning and part of an afternoon of no-result nymphing and dry fly fishing in The Channels of the Madison River in Montana. In that same afternoon, my longtime partner, as well as one of his local buddies well schooled in the technique, managed to haul in a mix of browns and rainbows in the two- to three-pound range—about a half-dozen each! I pleaded for some education, and here's what I got.

Start with the biggest, fattest, furriest, and most feathery fly you can imagine. Make sure it is also the *heaviest* fly that you can reasonably imagine. You throw out everything you have ever heard about graceful presentation, dead-drift nymph fishing, and the subtle take of a big fish.

Pick a spot with an opposite bank that is cast-accessible, or nearly so, one that has lots of rough water moving by it at a fair clip. The idea is to cast directly across stream, or to quarter upstream, placing your fly as close as you can to the bank. Of course, on the bank is just great too, as long as you can eventually get it off. Now comes the trickiest part, the part that is hardest for most of us to master—you do *nothing*. Nothing but hold tight, that is. Just let the big sweep of the rowdy current bow the line into a complete U, if it wants to, and sweep your fly downstream. Just stand there. Do nothing. Hold tight. After the flyline and leader are fully extended, strip your fly back to within three feet of you, then start again.

Since I once took a nasty line cut to the crease of my finger—the strike can be that fierce—it has been my habit to wrap a turn or two around my index and middle fingers. That way, my line is running out nowhere in those first few seconds as I set the hook and then ease the fish onto the reel.

For those of us who have spent years trying to finesse a nymph on the deadrift, this is an absolutely heretical way of angling. Instead of peering anxiously for that subtle hesitation or movement of line; instead of concentrating for the nearly imperceptible feel of the quick take-and-spit of a wise old lunker; instead of all that, you just hang tight. And hang on to your hat.

That afternoon, my seduction to this method of fishing was rapid and complete. After totally surrendering my prejudices, accepting a half-dozen of their outrageous flies, and doing as I was told, I started to catch fish. It was still pretty slow fishing. But, on what had been an absolutely deadly afternoon, I managed to turn several over and land a couple of fish. Nice fish. The real eye-opener for me that day was taking a beautiful two-pound brown out of a run that had just been fished six ways to Sunday by someone else. I watched the guy who preceded me. He could throw a pretty line and work a fly as sweetly as I've seen. He did a thirty- to forty-minute stint, using several flies. He went down, he went up, then down again. Nada. When he left, I nailed one on my very first ugly cast.

The final event, one that raised me from convert to zealot, occurred a couple of weeks later. Fulfilling my vow to import "ugly" to the Green Mountain State, I brought a three-pound rainbow to the net in my first hour of fishing.

I don't want to overstate the effectiveness of fishing ugly. You can receive as good a drubbing from the fishing gods using this method as well as any other. It is also true that, for anyone who loves throwing a dry fly around, a few hours of fishing ugly with no results is roughly equivalent to equal time in one of Dante's mid-range circles of Hell.

You see, the only fun part of this kind of fishing is catching the fish. The times when it is not producing fish are murderous. It is truly onerous work and has a built-in case of tendonitis for those of us over fifty. Anyone who enjoys the satisfaction of throwing a long line, of making a fly land on target, with grace and subtlety, should look elsewhere for entertainment. Ugly casting not only looks ugly, it feels ugly too. The flies that are used are so heavy that the distance you can hurl them is very limited. My nine foot for a five-weight is easily overpowered. In ugly fishing, a forty-foot cast comes with certifiable bragging rights. And, a word of caution—I would never attempt the technique without using at least some kind of glasses for eye protection. If you're doing it right, you will hit yourself on the back of the head regularly with the so-called flies. If "hard-hat nymphing" ever catches on in mass popularity, we can count on Orvis to offer a summer-weight vest with a ballistic nylon back. I'll welcome it. These little missiles have the weight of small lures, and they smart like hell wherever they tag you. And they *will* tag you.

Although I fish "ugly" flies in the trophy catch-and-release section of the Connecticut, it is because this stretch of the river can also be legally fished with hardware. I could not, in good conscience, use these in a fly-fishing-only environment. They are in reality small lures.

Now, you can tie any kind of ugly fly you want. I tie them on #2 - #4 streamer hooks with plenty of weight wrapped around the shanks. They all have produced, more or less, but there are a couple of standouts: the Black or Olive Wooly Bugger and "The Doctor."

The Wooly Bugger is a classic pattern. Tied ugly, they measure three to four inches from head to tail. If they splash loud enough to be audible above the rush of a fast moving stream, then you're getting them just about right.

"The Doctor" is a personal fly that was introduced to me on that fateful afternoon in the Madison's Channels. The friend of my friend, who gave me a half-dozen of these to start out my career, is the most prolific tyer I have ever known. According to his own estimate, on any given foray he packs some 1,500 flies. Counting the boxes of inventory he leaves in the car, he packs upwards of 7,000 flies for the week's fun. Thousands more reside at home. He ties scores of different patterns in different sizes. His favorites are tied two dozen deep.

Here's the irony. Over the course of the several trips we've shared, just about every damn time I ask him what he's using to catch fish—and he catches plenty of big fish—"The Doctor" is his response and mantra. Of course, I now fish it religiously too.

The Doctor is really based on a classic and now popular Western pattern, the Renegade. It is in effect a double, beadhead-Renegade. I usually use the biggest brass beadhead I can buy from the supply catalog. It has a peacock herl body, wound generously around a heavily weighted shank. After putting the beadhead on the hook, if I'm not feeling rushed, I'll start by wrapping a tag of tinsel at the bend of the hook. It stops the hackle from migrating back. Just for durability, I'll tie in a piece of metallic thread or fine wire to wrap it all down at the end. Add a few wraps of soft, chocolate brown hen hackle in front of the tag, working forward with peacock herl, a few wraps of white hackle

"The Doctor" — *Tail: none or gold tag; Body: peacock herl and wrapped gold wire; Hackle: brown to chocolate and white hen hackles; Head: beadhead (optional)*

at midpoint, some more herl, and a few more wraps of the chocolate hackle as the material approaches the back of the bead. Wrap the wire or metallic thread forward to nail it all down. Wrap up and tie it off, behind the beadhead. Dig out your safety glasses, and you're ready to fish ugly.

Leadeth Me Beside Still Waters

There is a powerfully hypnotic allure to the rise of a trout in water that is not moving. I hold a fully animated vision of one in my mind's eye. This fluid mandala of a pulsing rise in dark water, so full of promise and mystery, is the central metaphor for my love of stillwater trout fishing.

The rise of a trout in still water is entirely different from a rise in a brook or a stream. Sure, a pond trout can explode on a surface fly in a flashy take. Occasionally, they will even jump entirely free of their watery home to nail some airborne tidbit that has caught their dining fancy. Hell, sometimes you will see one jump and know that it's the sheer exuberance of being alive and swimming in the company of sister trout. The stillwater rise that is both more characteristic and more captivating, however, is a slow, deliberate take, just at the surface.

Compared to the urgent rises of trout in moving water, stillwater trout produce a more languorous and sensuous disturbance. In a stream, if the water is moving fast enough, the telltale ripple of a trout's meal will dissipate so quickly that you can begin to doubt that you even saw the rise in the first place. In a river, even the largest rise will immediately start to migrate downstream, dissolving quickly in the semi-chaos of the flow. Slam bam, thank you ma'am. On a lake or a pond, however, especially in the dark glassy water of an evening's slick, the rise of a trout lingers in the plane of the water's surface, pumping out perfectly concentric ripples. The length of the event seems interminable. Under the right conditions, you can watch a big trout take a natural fly under from a hundred feet away and track its radiating waves until they lap against your canoe like a friendly cat.

In these conditions, even a small trout can produce a rise that will set the heart racing. Fueled by the imagination, that rise becomes a slow motion tease, a taunting fingerprint of some multi-pound lunker. Oh boy, I love this kind of fishing. It was not always so.

There was a time when I could not even conceive of fishing for trout in a lake or a pond. Sure, these were great places to swim and, if they had a real beach, to meet girls. Or, if you absolutely had to, these were places to fish for bass, perch, pike, and whatever the hell else. They were not, however, the proper places to catch trout. Accepting my father's prejudice on the matter, lakes and ponds were the places that the people-who-liked-to-fish-with-a-forked-stick went. I was taught that this was no way to fish. Any real trouter worth their weight in twist-ons fished for trout in a proper stream. Coming from a guy who went to work in a tee-shirt all his life, it was a pretty aristocratic attitude.

It's still a common point of view. Especially common, I think, to those who prefer to use a fly. Like most prejudices, you really end up depriving yourself of rich company.

A few years ago, a non-fishing friend asked me to take him and his brother fishing. His brother still lived in their native California. He had just recently taken his fly-fishing-only vows. He was a convert on the heels of the Hollywood movie *A River Runs Through It*, and he was eager for some action while visiting the Green Mountain State. The rivers were running hot and low, but I knew of a spring-fed pond that had been very kind to me on the previous night. Since I had returned all the trout unharmed, and since conditions had been stable for the last eighteen hours, I thought that a return visit might be our best chance of getting some fish. When I suggested it, I might as well have farted in the middle of a submarine sermon. He curled his nose and demanded clear moving water. That evening we put in four hard hours on the Huntington River with only a little stinker or two to show for it. I know that we would have had some fun if my first suggestion had been accepted. Clear moving water is great, but it has its limitations.

Since that episode I've given in to being somewhat of a trout pond missionary, preaching the benefits of fishing for "land-bound" trout. My seduction to what some stream purists see as being coarser sport was not immediate. Over a period of years, however, I've moved from critic and skeptic to true believer. And it's not just the hypnotic power of the stillwater rise that has sold me on pond fishing. There are practical reasons for this love affair as well.

Reason one: The month of April (and sometimes some of May).

In Vermont, early season conditions on moving water can be tough on fly fishing. While spring rivers can run high and cold and have that look of diner coffee with 2% milk, lakes and ponds can offer hot fishing for those who can fish for brookies with midges, blue-wing olives, or a Mickey Finn. Early in the season, on some of the larger and deeper Vermont lakes, trolling or casting streamers will give a fly fisher a chance to take lakers and salmon up top, on light tackle. More than one opening-day skunking has been salvaged by a "side-trip" to a pond that was showing a little open water.

Although lakes and ponds offer refuge to the fly fisher predominantly in the early season, they also afford a welcome alternative to stream or river fishing *anytime* that the rivers go up. Given a ground saturation that is already high, a series of thunderstorms can put our larger rivers out of commission for a week or more. Although less common in July, August, or September, high muddy waters can visit throughout the summer. In fact, it seems to me that we lose a couple weeks or more of river fishing every summer due to these freshets. Jumping on the lakes and ponds is a way to keep on fishing.

And, oh yes, blackflies. Just as the trout fishing really starts to roll—in late May or early June in the northeast part of the state, earlier as you move south—blackflies make their appearance. Some historians have noted that the native Abenaki population would set up seasonal encampments on the shores of our lakes to take advantage of the breezes from the open water. They were definitely onto something good. Especially if you can get out on the water, you can escape this fly's most bloodthirsty rampages by thinning out their numbers. If the water is big enough and you can move your craft fast enough you can outrun them, then anchor down somewhere else. Far enough off shore and you're home free. Or you can fish closer to shore, having bought a little time before they find you again. June is the best of all seasons and fishing some open water can give you a break from its "dark side."

Besides adding about six or seven weeks to the flyfishing season and affording a seasonal respite from the scourge of blackflies, lakes and ponds also give the flyfisher a chance to take some bigger fish. This is especially true if you like to take your fish on dries. There is no question that the rivers produce whopping-size quarry, but most of the time it is bait or hardware that will win the day with these fish. Large river fish must maintain a finely tuned balance, one that weighs the nourishment gained from a meal against the effort expended in getting it. In most cases, flies just don't satisfy the formula. In still water, however, large trout can cruise ruthlessly, nearly effortlessly, taking stuff off the top at their whim. The largest river fish may become exclusive meat eaters, but in a lake or pond even the biggest trout will cruise the surface from time to time, reaping the bounty of some tasty insect fall. In these circumstances, those who love the dry fly move to equal footing with the metal and meat folk.

How about vistas? The open sky views that attend a visit to a lake or pond are another attraction. In no way would I disparage the beauty of rivers and streams, with their pools and falls, cutting through the cool green forest. There are spectacularly scenic river valleys, edged by mountain skylines, that would not take second place in any contest of scenery. But there is something special about the open sky vistas provided by a lake or pond. They produce in me a wonderful sense of expanse, very similar to that achieved on the top of a mountain. Whether I'm emerging from the woods to the edge of a ten-acre backwoods pond or taking in a near-360-degree view of a mountain-dominated horizon from the shore of a Lake Champlain island, there is an exhilaration to the scene that is not there for me in the bend of the river, nor under the shady canopy of a winding stream, nor in the claustrophobic rush of water through a gorge. Lakes and ponds give you a seat right on Nature's fifty-yard line.

Wildlife, especially larger birds and raptors, are more evident around these water bodies. There are also improved chances at seeing some of our larger mammals, like moose or deer. Then there is *wilderness.* Do you like the idea of getting a few miles away from civilization to fish for trout? Well, if that appeals, it is only our small backwoods ponds that will offer anything like a wilderness experience. Moreover, we only have about a score of these to count and about half as many to boast about. In Vermont, the roads follow our rivers and streams, and after nearly two and a half centuries of development, it is only the smallest of our brooks that run through unbroken forest. So, if you really want to "get back there" and catch some decent sized trout, you'll have to find yourself a trout pond.

In the end, I think that the real reasons for my love affair with this kind of fishing are emotional. Some of the allure is the mystery. Still waters are more inscrutable. They can't be read as easily as the currents and eddies of a river or a brook. The distribution of the fish seems entirely more random. In fact, there is rhyme and reason as to where fish may lie and feed, but it is a lot harder to dope out in these habitats than in moving water. Looking at its surface, a lake or pond will usually present the angler with a faceless plane that may be hundreds of acres in extent and essentially uniform in appearance. Without knowledge of the subsurface, one anonymous unidentifiable patch of water looks just like the next. It presents an immediate challenge, a puzzle to be solved . . . a mystery.

Lakes and ponds are also wildly capricious. Surely the god of stillwater trout is first cousin to Janus, the two-faced god that ruled gateways and doors during the heyday of the Roman empire. When the Romans were at war, his temple doors were left open; when peace prevailed, they were closed. Just succumb to a little overconfidence in your ability to wage war on your favorite stillwater fishing hole and the governing demigod will turn its back on you, slam the doors shut, and show you the poker face that resides on the back of its smile.

In whatever lake or pond you're fishing there seems to be an ever-present, and in the end unpredictable, "on/off switch." This "switch" seems to hold sway over these water bodies. Although I have an ultimate faith that this on/off feature is strictly governed by physical realities—like the sudden availability of a food source or the migrations of a feeding pod of trout—when that switch is thrown, one way or the other, it seems to have more to do with magic than with science. After hours of stripping wet flies without success, all of a sudden you start to take one fish after another. One minute the trout are hitting at every cast, minutes later you can't buy a hit. Or you've been trolling hitless for the better part of a day and, on the edge of losing hope, you find yourself in the middle of surface feeding frenzy with trout jumping everywhere. It can be crazy.

In fishing a hospitable stream or a river, it is rare that an experienced fly fisher can't pound up at least a couple small trout for a day's efforts. A lake or pond will offer no such quarter. Under the poorest circumstances, you can go for days without taking a single fish. It can be daunting fishing.

It can also be trout bedlam, with a multitude of fish breaking the surface and taking everything you throw at them. A healthy lake can explode with quantities of large feeding trout. Find yourself fishing in the right place at the right time, and you can be onto what is, for my money, the most exciting trout fishing that there is. My idea of heaven is fishing an eternal evening slick, the dark surface of its water erupting here and there from the attentions of very large brook trout. They make huge, slow motion suck-holes in its placid surface. Each rise looks like some unseen hand has pulled the plug out of the bottom of the pond and threatens to drain it.

To be sure, heaven does happen in this world from time to time, but it is fleeting. When it does happen I'm reduced to the state of an excited young man, blissfully in the throes of what any psychologist would agree to be a "peak experience."

Secrets to Big Brookies
(and Lakers too)

My father's routine method for fishing stream trout was to use a worm on a small Eagle Claw spinner. He maneuvered this surf-and-turf combo with an eight-foot bamboo fly rod and was seldom denied.

But, on those times when he was foiled in producing a strike, he would resort to a unique array of alternative "baits." Grubs, grasshoppers, caterpillars, fish eyes or fins from some coarse fish, leaches, dobsons, newts or salamanders — all worked well for him. He also claimed brilliant success with such things as apple skins, cigarette butts, wild strawberries, pieces of cloth, and even the old-style, removable pop-top rings from a can of beer. He maintained that brookies favored Schlitz. I think it was he, however, who favored the Schlitz. The brookies took what they were offered.

I have more or less confirmed the efficacy of all of the above, and I could add a few of my own. One of my dearest child-hood memories was hiking miles up a small tributary of the upper Connecticut River and taking a fine catch of squaretails on small pieces of stew beef. Subsequently, I have personally witnessed great fish succumb to an array of oddities, ranging from lug nuts to fried chicken.

The chicken produced one of the largest brookies I've ever seen taken out of a Vermont pond. It fell prey to a #00 Chicken McNugget. It was fished slow and deep by the six-year-old daughter of a friend. That brookie was sixteen inches long and fat as a crippled capon. And, just to prove that her McFishing technique was no fluke, the young lady caught a twelve-incher a few minutes later. These were the only two trout we saw during an entire day of fishing.

The absolute strangest method for catching trout—you judge for yourself—relates to taking big lakers. It was told to me by an old salt I met in Averill. He claimed it was surefire and would produce trophy lake trout when all else fails.

You need the following to start out with: an old cigar box, some paint, a 500-foot spool of strong packing twine, a hefty casting rod rigged with several hundred feet of twenty-pound-test line, two medium rubber bands, four treble hooks, four steel leaders, a fresh alder twig, a handful of shelled walnuts, and a large washer ring.

With a pen knife, completely and carefully remove the lid of the cigar box and paint its outside half red and half white. Paint the entire inside green.

Using the knife again, cut a small slit in the exact middle of one of its long sides. Make it just large enough to fit the diameter of the washer ring. Tie the twine to the washer. Stick the washer ring halfway in the slit, then jam the alder twig through the half of the washer which emerges inside the box.

Rig each of the treble hooks to a steel leader and then tie the four leaders off the end of the twenty-pound-test line. Divide the leader-hook combinations into two pairs. Place one rubber band around each of these pair of leader-hook combinations, so it will hold fast to what you will later attach there.

You are now ready to wait for a day, close to ice-out, when there is a steady breeze blowing out from the shore.

You get a lively chipmunk and secure a pair of treble hooks on each end, using the rubber bands. One of these harnesses goes around its neck, the other around its waist. Arrange all of the hooks so they hang from the chipmunk's flanks, taking care that they don't interfere with its legs.

Place the chipmunk in the box and add the walnuts. You set the box adrift and play out both the packing twine and the fishing line as the box is blown away from the land. It's painted red and white on the outside, so you can see it for a long way off. The green inside—along with the walnuts, of course—has a calming effect on the rodent, so it doesn't go and capsize the box prematurely.

When you have played out nearly all the packing twine, you give it one hell of a yank and wind the capsized, empty box in as fast as you can—it can be used again.

It is well known that big muskellunge have an earned reputation for predation on unwary ducks. The sport from Averill assured me that the sight and sound of a half-pound chipmunk, thrashing and chattering in the water, is more than early-season lakers can stand. Even the biggest and most canny will fall prey to this ploy.

Now you might ask, like I did, as to where the hell you come by the chipmunk. He said that's the easy part. You get an old one-quart mayonnaise jar, a spool of blue yarn . . .

The Averill Lakes

Great Averill Pond once served me up an extraordinary afternoon of trout fishing. It was a near cloudless day. The water was clear as acetone and frigid. Although the lake rippled here and there with errant and short-lived breezes, it remained about as flat a piece of afternoon water that one could ever hope to see. In early May's shadeless sunshine, I was dizzy and hot-faced with the season's very first sunburn, and, oh boy, the trout were hitting.

I was hooking one every third or fourth cast. By my humble standard, which still respects an eight-inch brookie, they were nice trout indeed. One behemoth of unknown size had broken me off, and the ones I was managing to land were running between thirteen and sixteen inches long. They were lake trout, and the fact that they were decidedly short of legal size did little to undermine this day as one of my most memorable fishing experiences. I was catching these "beefy brookies" on fine tippet, casting small wet flies—from shore, no less. In fact, the clarity of the water in the thirty-foot-deep shoal I was attending was such that you could see the fish on their strike-run, moving faster

31

than I ever conceived lakers could move. All the fish, of course, were quickly returned to their chilly home waters.

Great Averill Pond and its neighbor, Little Averill Pond, rank high in the pantheon of Vermont fishing holes. The "Averill lakes," as they are commonly referred to in the collective, are large, deep, and very cold. They are among only a handful of Vermont lakes that might be scientifically classified as "oligo-trophic" lakes. Little changed from the days when the glaciers retreated to the north, these waters remain highly oxygenated coldwater reservoirs, virtually barren of subaqueous plant life. Nestled deep in the Northeast Kingdom at the edge of a vast tract of spruce-fir forest, they are located at the perimeter of one of Vermont's wildest areas. They surely rank among the crown jewels of Vermont's coldwater fishery.

Although it's just a hop, skip, and jump to the Connecticut River, the waters of this part of Vermont actually drain north, into the St. Lawrence River. For me, both of these deepwater lakes have always had a special romance. In large part this is based on the widely accepted account that they were the last domain of Vermont's very own species of golden trout. Accord-ing to some, these fish are the taxonomic relatives of the Sunapee trout family of New Hampshire. Having honed my appreciation of golden trout elsewhere, it has always been a pleasant fantasy to imagine one of those Vermont goldens mak-ing a surprising reappearance on the end of my line.

Little Averill Pond is located just over three miles south of the Canadian border, in the town of Averill. It is reached by driving east, out of Norton, along Route 114. The drive paral-lels the U.S.-Canada international boundary, and every time I have made this pilgrimage I can't help thinking to myself, "This is the very top of Vermont!" My position on the road map, the steady climb out of Norton and the Coaticook River valley, as well as the anticipation of hot fishing, all combine to support this illusion of being "on top." Hell, maybe it's not an illusion at all. It's fishing for the fat-and-sassy rainbows—and for lake trout that give even revered Willoughby a run for its money—that make this lake one of the most exciting angling destinations in the state. And, as if great fishing wasn't enough, Little Averill Pond adjoins a near-wilderness setting that is host to abundant wildlife and fine scenery. Moose abound, the loons seem to be holding their own and, at least on either side of summer, there's a chance to see osprey above its waters. From the lake's southern end the view of Brosseau Mountain's sheer crags is in itself enough to justify any excursion to this part of the planet, regardless of the results in the fish department.

From where Averill Creek crosses under the paved highway, Route 114, a logging road comes in on the right (south). Follow it as it parallels the shore of Great Averill Pond, heading southeast for about two and a half miles. Then it bends around, heading southwest. Stay with it and, in another half mile, the public boat access is marked by a sign on your left. Although the boat ramp at Little Averill can accommodate trailer launches easily, the three miles of logging road that access it aren't always as willing. The road can get soupy enough to require four-wheel drive, especially in the spring.

I've always loved launching from this access. It is in a sheltered, narrow neck of water that leads to the main body of the lake. At times this sheltered stretch of water can produce some great dry fly fishing. As your craft enters the broad lake from this sheltered neck, your line of sight runs over a mile-and-a-half of open water. To the south and west is a great expanse of undeveloped shoreline. It is big water, and permission to fish is granted by the weather it serves up.

My very first visit was nearly twenty years ago, and I remember the change in weather even more clearly than I do the great fishing. A gale quickened so unexpectedly that it was terrifying. In our small, underpowered aluminum boat, we had absolutely no shot at winning the mile-long race to the boat access. Within the space of ten or fifteen minutes we were in it thick. The blue water—calm enough to allow us to stalk and catch rising salmon with streamers—had turned battleship gray and become a writhing field of whitecaps. With the water temperature in the low fifties and no other craft in sight, a mishap would have led to a ready case of hypothermia at best.

In the end, of course, we arrived safely back at the access. It was only when our knees stopped shaking that we complained about getting blown out of some of the fastest salmon fishing we'd ever encountered. Nowadays the salmon, a noble experiment of our fishery biologists, are gone.

Little Averill Pond is a glacially gouged lake that lies in the high valley formed between the flanks of Brousseau and Green Mountain. This area is the northern limit of the state's Northeastern Highlands, a mountain range that is geologically unrelated to the Green Mountains. Instead, the base rock here is raw, plutonic granite. Except for the cooling and the weathering, the rock remains pretty much as it was when it oozed up from the bowels of the earth. These mountains are actually part of New Hampshire's White Mountains system. Immediately to the south is the vast and undeveloped Nulhegan Basin, a twenty-thousand-acre tract of spruce-fir forest and cedar swamp, guarded by rugged mountains all around. It is a land of pointed trees, loggers, and fishin'-huntin' kind of folk. This region is just about as wild as it gets in Vermont.

Little Averill Pond is an anachronism that harkens back to prehistoric Vermont. It was then that those "golden trout" and the lakers got themselves stranded, as the post-glacial earth rebounded and ocean retreated. Its bottom is barren rock and sand. The food chain here is simple, with lake trout and rainbows on the top. Smelt, crustaceans, and insects scattered throughout their great depths sustain the larger fish.

A couple of years ago, some non-fishing friends accompanied me on a visit. I had touted the clarity of the water, so they brought their scuba gear. After donning wet suits and adjusting their regulators for what is technically a high elevation dive (the elevation is 1,740 feet), they spent forty-five minutes or so exploring while I went fishing. When they returned I was expecting them to bubble with the same romance with which I regard this water. Instead, they complained that although it was an unusually clear lake, it afforded a pretty boring dive.

With an average depth of more than fifty feet and a maximum depth of 115 feet, Little Averill Pond would be classified among Vermont's deeper lakes. Its clarity is due to its lack of bottom vegetation. It is a thrill to troll or cast a streamer fly and see a streak of silver emerge from the depths to strike. I have also seen yard-long lakers skulking along the bottom in twenty feet of water, some right in the sheltered neck of the boat access. And it has been at those times that I found myself wishing for a spinning rod and a multi-ounce lure that could get down to them quick enough.

From my observation of those piloting the bigger rigs, a favorite trolling lane is a swoop of the southern and western perimeter of the lake. The lakers seem to come from the thirty- to forty-foot depths in the early part of the season, running deeper as the water warms up. In recent years Little Averill has been under special regulations. A minimum length and re- duced limits on rainbows and a much restricted season on lak- ers, including establishment of a twenty-four-inch minimum length, are going to do nothing but more good things for this place. You can count on special management for years to come, so check the current regulations. Although most of the fish- ing attention tends to be focused on the lakers, it can offer good fly fishing for rainbows throughout the season.

When you're up in this part of the world, Forest Lake de- mands a visit. I used to fish it as a fall-back spot to the Averills, but it has now become a destination point in its own right. At about one-fifth the size of Little Averill Pond, it has a much smaller fetch than its neighbors and so is a little kinder to small boats. When the weather comes from the west, it gets a little protection from the small hill that rises a few hundred feet above it. As a result it's a good place to try if the wind is howl- ing on the Averills. (Another good alternative when the wind is up is Averill Creek. It's a great place to do the kind of fishing that nurtured my youth—bait fishing with worms in the deep holes in the pool-falls-pool-type of brook that characterizes steep terrain. The occasional ten-inch brookie Averill Creek offers makes it a worthwhile sidetrip.)

While large boats and large motors are fine—one might even say demanded—on the Averills, such equipment is totally inappropriate here on Forest Lake. This is a shallow and weedy little piece of heaven. With a maximum depth that probably doesn't exceed twenty feet, it is in studied contrast with its neighbors. But it is every bit the fishing jewel. If the Averills are sapphires or emeralds, Forest Lake is precious amber. It holds vicious brown trout, unquestionably some of the prettiest I've seen. They come in both jaw-dropping color and size. I recently saw a brown break the surface for a natural caddis fly. Its head was the size of my hand!

To get to Forest Lake, go east on Route 114 and make the first right after the shore road on Great Averill, about a quarter-mile from the Averill Store. Follow signs to "Quimby Country." In a mile and a half the road forks. To the right there is a short stretch of public road and a small, cartop-carry boat access.

If you're feeling flush in the wallet, continue down the right-hand road to "Quimby Country" and stay (reservations!) at a hundred-year-old fishing camp that has evolved to become a unique family resort. Before the family season, in the early spring through the peak of the blackflies, Quimby's remains the exclusive domain of fishing folk, offering superb hospitality, funky classic camp digs, and a boat or two on the lakes in the vicinity.

If you catch the season just right on a Sunday morning, you will witness a parade of cars containing locals from Norton and Canaan. They are beating a path to a buffet breakfast of widespread reputation. It opens to the non-guest public only a few times a year, just before the camp opens its family season. This whopper of a feed has been tweaked to perfection by the responses of hungry visitors over the last hundred fishing seasons or so. It is a mid-morning brunch that will set you up right for the rest of the day. (Call to confirm availability.)

As far as fishing flies are concerned, there are three or four that come to the forefront as my all-time producers on these (as well as other Northeast Kingdom) lakes.

In the early season a Gray Ghost, trolled or cast, is a good bet on all three lakes. This fly, which has been around since before Quimby Country broke ground, is the traditional smelt imitation for northern New England lakes. Although there are no smelt in Forest Lake, the fly works well on the browns, which earn their reputation of preferring "meat" once they are of size. Of course the fly is in its natural element on the larger lakes. While the water remains cold, lakers may be taken at relatively shallow depths. My standard offerings, when casting or trolling up top, are store-bought #6 - #10, 6X-long streamers. For trolling with a weighted line, larger tandem versions are a good bet. Tied with standard or short-shanked hooks, #0 - #4, they can range up to five or six inches long.

The fly that was kind to me, the one that served up the succession of small lakers on that hot May afternoon, was a weighted #14 magenta "grub." It is the height of simplicity to tie—a tag of black thread, body of magenta floss, that's it. This fly, which was created solely because of prompting by my (then) four-year-old daughter, has had a hallowed spot in my wallet since. It readily dives down six to eight feet and has scored on everything from brookies to salmon.

Another fly that is a sporadic but impressive winner is a large cinnamon/dark amber ant. Once you've seen a proper hatch of "timber ants," you're not likely to be without at least one of these in your arsenal. One of these ant-falls is something to behold. The number of three- and four-pound rainbows that can be provoked into action is startling. These ants are the better part of an inch long and sport a set of crystal wings that, given the fact that hundreds and perhaps thousands of these ants are dropping helplessly into the lake, seem patently ineffective. In addition to the size of the meal it represents for the efficiency-minded larger trout, the struggling of the insect in surface film causes commotion enough to excite even jaded lunkers. In fishing the fly I like to alternate a minute or so of twitching it carefully in the film with a few minutes of letting it lie dead still. As with other flies I fish like this, I very often get my strike in the first few twitches after a period of repose.

My personal all-time producer for big stillwater rainbows is a wing-less hare's ear, tied as a "Wiggle-Nymph." Fished slow and deep, it has

shown me some of my best times. I was first introduced to this fly in 1971 in Selective Trout *by Swisher and Richards. It is the only fly of theirs that I persist in fishing. The Wiggle Nymph is a jointed fly, but aside from that, it is a simple pattern to tie. On a straight-eye, #12 wet fly hook, start to tie a standard hare's ear—soft brown hackle for tail, tan fur body from the ear, and gold ribbing. When the body is finished, immediately tie off the head, whip finish, and lacquer. With wire cutters, cut off the entire rear section of the hook, from the start of the bend, just back from where the tail meets hook. This little piece is the hookless, rear segment of the nymph. Thread the eye of this rear section with an inch or two of fine "gold" wire. Now drop a #12 short-shanked hook into your vise. Lay down a layer of thread on it and tie on the fold of gold wire, which is now holding the "wiggle" part of the nymph. Tie it close, but not tight up against the front section. Leave enough of the wire loop and a little space so that the rear section can move freely. Trim the excess wire and finish the fly with a fur body and gold ribbing. You can add a soft brown hackle if you want. In either case pluck at the fur just behind the head to create the classic throat-hackle of the hare's ear.*

Wiggle Nymph — Tail: brown hen hackle; Body: fur from a hare's mask; Hackle: brown hen hackle; Head: brown thread.

The Key to Paradise

Part One

Yes, the trout god can giveth and taketh—and even bringeth back again. One grand day, about twenty years ago, she did all three, at least for my companion.

Now there was a certain Burlington councilman who, long before he launched his political career, prevailed upon me to take him fishing. To preserve this Democrat's (whoops!) anonymity, we'll call him Mr. M.

"Show me a little something," said Mr. M.

"O.K.," says I, "Monday, 4 a.m. sharp."

But wait. Before I launch into this story, there is another tale that precedes it by some five years. Telling it will provide a sort of extended preface. It also reveals a little of the quality of my planned destination for Mr. M, and why it was (and still is) such a secret.

The place to which I am referring lies somewhere in the Northeast Kingdom, a drive and then some from Lyndonville.

The "then some" is a brisk forty-five minute walk along a rug-ged, four-wheel-drive road. I walked in the very first time I dis-covered this little acre of paradise and have made it a point to walk in ever since.

The reason for my steadfast behavior is simple: stealth. My first arrival was not by road but through the woods, using a compass. It was by this alternate route that I managed to avoid the multitude of POSTED signs that herald along the pond's more conventional approach. These signs bristle along the access road as well as the west side of the pond. It is this side that hosts a small, well-kept camp. On the bushwhack route that I first took, I saw not a single sign.

On that inaugural day I was in the company of three friends. We all were three-quarters of the way to our bag limits before we saw the first no-trespass sign. We were young and brash then. Not only were we a few years away from being captivated by the idea of catch-and-release, we were sometimes willing to walk the fine line on matters of trespass . . . if the fishing was good enough. We therefore quickly reasoned that some variant of a grandfather clause was operative. We were there already. We nearly had our limits. So why not stay and finish what we started?

In a little while everyone but yours truly had their full limit. All in all, they were as healthy a set of brook trout as you would ever hope to lay your eyes on. I had been keeping myself open for a twelfth fish. I was aspiring to a real lunker, one to surpass the brace of foot-long beasts that joined nine lesser brethren in my creel. As time came to head home, the four of us con-gregated to clean the fish before hiking out.

When all the trout were piled together, we went to cleaning them in an assembly-line fashion. Before we could pack up the day's catch, however, two game wardens materialized out of nowhere. Given the enormous pile of trout they were seeing, they were confident they had nabbed four ruthless poachers and were none too friendly. One demanded licenses while the other began a methodical count of the fish.

As to ourselves, we were not at all concerned about being within the law, at least as far as licenses and bag limits were concerned. We knew that each of us would have attended to the business of buying a license and keeping an exact count of his catch. We were very concerned, however, as to how our presence on posted land might play.

"Forty-seven fish," one of the wardens announced.

We were one trout shy of the legal limit. After being briefly challenged on the fact that our respective catches should have technically been kept in the individual possession of each angler, they relented. We explained that they indeed had been until we amassed them for cleaning. Then, anticipating a further challenge regarding the postings, we began to explain that we hadn't seen the signs because we came at the pond from the other direction.

By now the wardens were beginning to warm up to us, no doubt because we had been exceedingly deferential. It was also clear that we had effectively and precisely policed ourselves though we were miles from the nearest paved road.

"Well, to tell the truth, these postings aren't legal," one of them allowed. "The state stocks the pond, and it *is* open to fishing."

As we parted company with the wardens, we could hardly contain our joy. We began our march out, this time by the road. The wardens stayed behind. They wanted to fish too, no doubt.

What a find! As we hiked, we congratulated ourselves on the discovery and began to think it through. Given the multitude of posted signs along the road to the pond, we loathed the idea of ever confronting the owner of the camp. Imagine trying to support our presence there by referring to the "authoritative ruling" we had just received from the wardens. No, that wouldn't do. We had to be extremely careful. We agreed to the following:

  a) not tell anyone else
  b) lest the name slip our lips, we would always refer to it as "Paradise Pond"
  c) that we would keep future visitation to a minimum
  d) never visit on the weekend

Years have passed since that first visit and, except for bringing Mr. M, I have stuck religiously to the rules we set. I have revisited it many times, usually only once in a season, never more than twice. I have had a skunking or two there, but Paradise Pond has proved that the results of that very first encounter were no accident.

I have never seen the owner of the camp.

Part Two

"OK. This is it. Forty-five minutes to Paradise Pond," I announced to Mr. M. I parked at what would be our trailhead, and we began to unload the car.

Now I truly despise that minority of materialistic anglers who are as much into their tackle or dress as they are into their sport, but Mr. M's fishing outfit cannot pass without comment.

Excalibur was a one-piece, all-metal bait casting rod, clearly too old to have been a first-generation possession. Though a bit bent and rusted from tip to haft, it promised another fifty years of service. His reel was mismatched to the rod. It was a closed-face spinning type of some cheap 1950s manufacture. Such as it was, it was permanently affixed to the reel seat by means of several pounds of electrical tape. Shredded black and gray threads hung down in abundance from the aging tape. All in all, it looked much like a small, dull-colored jellyfish was trying to digest the lower half of Mr. M's rod.

The reel was filled with ten-pound-test nylon line. The latter had no doubt resided on the reel for several generations. When he unfurled it to thread the only two remaining guides on the rod, it displayed enough memory curls to excite even the most world-weary of Slinky toys.

The hook, which he tied on with a dozen square knots, was a double-0 Mustad. From my perspective it was really more appropriate for gaffing a trout caught on a smaller hook.

Mr. M told me he had a container of worms in the plastic tackle box that accompanied him. At that point, I could only conjecture as to what else might reside in the box. As I indicated, I wasn't at all smug in these observations, but merely concerned that I might later have to share my own tackle in order to let Mr. M bag some trout. Never was a concern so misplaced.

The walk in was pleasant in the cool morning air. Here and there a patch of ground fog gave the passing forest landscape an eerie appearance, an aspect reinforced by the hooting of a tenacious barred owl who refused to call it a night. We jumped a deer and a few sleepy partridge. As we made our final approach to the pond, we passed no less than a half-dozen signs. KEEP OUT. NO TRESPASSING. POSTED. PRIVATE PROPERTY. Mr. M became more than a little distressed. I assured him, however, that I had it on the highest authority that the admonitions were merely the groundless prattle of an overwrought and mean-spirited landowner.

When we arrived at the pond, it was flat as a bedsheet. The camp was vacant.

We made our way around to the small inlet on the far side and set up our tackle. When he opened his box, I tactfully steered Mr. M into substituting his only #6 snelled Eagle Claw for the tarpon hook that he had tied on earlier. He had no sinkers or shot, so he affixed a small bobber and was in business . . . more or less.

Mr. M stayed put, but I flyfished my way around the entire pond over the course of the next two hours. As I joined him for a mid-morning lunch, I reported that I had got only a couple of short strikes for my efforts. He related how, in trying to cast his rig, he had whipped his entire supply of garden worms off the hook.

"As hard as I'd cast it, I couldn't get any more than ten feet or so. Are you sure there are fish in here?" he interrogated me.

I assured him that not only were there fish but it was probably the best piece of standing trout water, in its size class, in all of northern Vermont. He was unimpressed.

Mr. M concluded that he simply was not getting the distance he needed with his casting. He started to rummage through his tackle box. It soon became apparent that small bobbers were his forte. One might say he was a small bobber specialist. He must have had fifteen or twenty of them, white-red, yellow-red, red-white, red-yellow. Next in plenitude was his medley of colossal hooks—the double-0 hand-hammered Mustad was mid-range in size. Then there were bottles of pork rind (in three colors) and salmon eggs (four colors), all pick-led in formaldehyde. He had thousands of feet of spinning line, on several spools. None were less than ten-pound-test. Mr. M was not about to run short of fishing line or break off anything smaller than a tuna. There was also some assorted junk, added, I thought, to improve the box's rattle.

He pondered this array for an interminable length of time, then made his move. His selection: an old-fashioned "church key" with the word "Schaefer" engraved in cursive along the hilt. It was four or five inches long and apparently had the heft that Mr. M was looking for. He expertly ran his line through the holes near each end and tied on a rusty #4 hook. (If he didn't land any trout he hooked, he at least would kill it with lockjaw.) With his new lure swinging ponderously from the end of his rod, he approached the water's edge. He whipped the rod in a vicious arc, and the "lure" whistled through the air for the better part of a hundred feet, like a World War II bomb. KERSPLASH!

He was about two cranks into the retrieve when his rod bent heavily in response to the strike of a large trout. "Oh Boy!" he screamed, and the fight was on. With ten-pound-test connect-ing him and the brookie, the contest was decided as soon as it had begun. In a couple of minutes he had a fat thirteen-incher at his feet.

I stood in amazement, offering him compliments on his angling insight. Whizzzzz . . . KERSPLASH . . . two cranks . . . his metal pole arced again in response to another fish. Its flashy acrobatics woke me up from my envious reverie. *Let's get fish-ing. They're starting to hit.* I walked down the shore a polite dis-tance and, with hands shaking, tied on a big Gray Ghost. I was soon working the water feverishly with the streamer. He was already onto his third fish, which, judging from the commotion it was causing and the bend of his rod, was the largest so far. I finished my tenth cast. My twentieth. I could not buy a single hit.

Meanwhile Mr. M could hardly maneuver that can opener through six feet of water without a trout tearing into it. I could hear him cuss and laugh as he missed several strikes. He was dropping some fish after they were on as well, but in less than thirty minutes time he had acquired a respectable pile of brookies at his feet.

I tried a few casts with three or four other flies, also with negative results. Finally I gave up, reeled in, and walked back to watch my companion do his thing. He was smirking, and he had earned it. He had another fish on. With the distraction of my arrival he mistakenly allowed this last one to sound deep.

"Judas priest!" He had let the trout snag him up on the bottom. He leaned into the rod several times. The line twanged and hummed each time he pulled it taut, but the lure, and presumably the trout on the end, did not budge. At length, he decided to cut the line.

"Well, that was quite a show," I said, perhaps a little relieved that, with the loss of the can-opener, my humiliation had run its course. Boy, was I wrong again. Mr. M opened his tackle box, explored and rattled around in its depths, and at length produced another eccentric selection: the lug nut from a car wheel.

He quickly secured it to the line and tied another large hook to it. I was no longer a doubter. I sat and watched in anticipation. Whizzzzzz . . . KACHOOK! It landed like a depth charge.

A few cranks of the reel and, there he was, onto another large fish! This one ran him high and low, hung him up on the bottom for a minute or so, and then reluctantly came ashore under the relentless haul of Mr. M's right arm and his ten-pound-test. As the fish flopped to his feet, both of our jaws dropped in amazement. There, in a thirty-foot tangle of curled nylon, was the Schaefer church key he had cut free just a few minutes ago.

Because the hook attached to the Schaefer opener was not set in this fourteen-inch brookie's mouth, it was impossible to say for sure whether it was a case of the same trout hitting twice or if the second trout just became entangled with the lost lure. Whatever the case, it was clear that it was Mr. M's day and that he was to be denied nothing.

I broke down my own rod and just sat and watched as he worked his final magic. He continued casting for another ten or fifteen minutes and caught the few other trout he needed to fill a limit.

By noon we were back at the car. Even though I had taken a conspicuous skunking, that day will always be one of my most memorable fishing excursions. One of his too, no doubt.

Back in Burlington, we stopped at Kerry's store on St. Paul Street. He treated to a six-pack of Schaefer. When we got to his house he broke a couple out of the carton and, ignoring their pop-tops, cracked them open with the very same church key that unlocked Paradise.

A Creature of the Night

Since a good fly line is a pricey piece of tackle, and the circumstances in which you are forced to cut one are so very rare, such an event will not likely be forgotten. And so now, even twenty years after that fateful evening, my recollection of it has the clarity of a late-summer brook.

A seasoned fishing partner and I had planned a hike-in fishing trip to a small pond in the southern Green Mountains. We would camp overnight. It was mid-July, and we knew from experience that hexagenia would be hatching there. A hatch of these colossal mayflies can turn a healthy body of trout water into a three-ring circus . . . but more on that later.

On the evening before our departure we were paid an unexpected visit by a dear friend and former schoolmate, Jack. He had driven all the way up from New Jersey to surprise us. Jack was a city boy. Shortly after graduation, he abandoned the green hills of Vermont for the Jersey Shore. There, he had ready access to those urban amenities he felt indispensable, most of all the thoroughbred races at Monmouth Park. For Jack, horse racing bordered on obsession. As he liked to put it, "You can screw anytime, but the daily double is at one o'clock."

He was now a bartender and seldom saw the morning sun. He lived in a small studio apartment. He never even lit the stove, taking all his meals out. Daily at noon, he could be seen on his hike to the local hash house where he would buy a "'tainer" of coffee, a couple of bagels, and a copy of the *Morning Telegraph*.

A true flatlander's flatlander, Jack was not a likely candidate for our planned hike. As for a night's sleep on cold earth . . . well, his idea of "roughing it" was drinking beer in the grandstand instead of sipping cognac in the clubhouse.

We also shared a certain history. He had given trout fishing a fair try before. This same fishing partner and I brought him out on a fishing trip to Parc Mauricie in southern Quebec. Sometimes it's the obvious that gets overlooked, and often to ill consequence. This was a June trip, and the blackflies were rampant. Although we had taken pains to coach him well on his casting and given him an ample supply of bug dope, we failed to utter one word about *tucking his pant legs into his socks*.

The blackflies had at his legs in the worst way. After a day's fishing, his ankles and calves were bloodied. We compounded our oversight by not emphasizing that he had to take care with his scratching. A few days after his return to Vermont, the bites became infected. Everything turned out okay, but his ankles were to bear indelible scars.

Nevertheless, our planned trip to the hexagenia in the southern Greens had the momentum of a tractor trailer on a downhill—there was no way in hell we would reschedule. We poured three fingers of Metaxa brandy in each of three snifters, drew a breath, and launched our pitch. "This is great timing, Jack . . . you'll see some real backcountry fishing . . . the walk in is no hump at all . . . great trail . . . right on the flat . . . we've got all the equipment you need . . . just bring your toothbrush."

Immediately Jack had both trouser legs rolled up to midcalf and socks peeled down. He was swearing a blue streak and stabbing his fingers at the smallpox-like scars that wreathed his pale ankles. "No friggin' way, guys!"

Despite the energy of his initial protests, by the time we finished the Metaxa he gave grudging assent. We had promised him everything—carrying the packs, cooking the meals, doing the dishes, great fishing, and no bugs. In retrospect, it is difficult to say whether it was our deft arguments or his genuine desire for our fellowship that made our case. When we played our final card, however, it was in terms that he well understood: "Look, Jack, you can visit anytime but that mayfly hatch is tomorrow night at eight o'clock."

Given the Metaxa and late bedtime, morning came early. Surprisingly, the final preparations were promptly accomplished, and we managed a decent departure time. The drive to civilization's edge—in Danby—passed quickly, and before long we were on the trail. Two of us carried all the trip's necessities in fifty-pound packs. It was a spectacular summer day.

Jack, looking every bit like he expected to find a Greyhound bus terminal within the next hundred feet, carried a few personal items in a small gym bag. He wore pressed casual slacks and a knit shortsleeve shirt. On his head was a straw porky-pie hat with a bright madras band. Around his neck, in a grand gesture to this outdoor adventure, he carried his racetrack binoculars. Ensconced in a hard leather case, they were better than a foot wide and weighed about five pounds.

All said and done he did give a good accounting of himself on the trail. In fact, since he carried no pack, we found ourselves looking at his back for most of the hike.

After arrival and camp set-up, Jack spent the afternoon reading a paperback while we pounded the pond's choppy water with a variety of wet flies. No luck. We returned to camp to find Jack snoozing peacefully. He was enjoying himself.

We broke for a late afternoon snack, then gave Jack refresher drills in casting, tying knots, and so on. And, of course, we tried to work him up a little about the foot-long brookies that we knew lurked deep in the clear waters of the pond. There are sixteen- to eighteen-inch bruisers in there as well.

As the sun started to dip low, we all headed to the south side of the pond, which had several exceptional places where you could cast a long line from shore. We selected the very best spot for Jack. I tied on a Blue-winged Olive for him to start with, admonishing him to change over to the larger flies once he saw the hexagenia hatching. I gave him a half-dozen #10 store-bought Muddlers and a single copy of my own hex imitation. Cast dry and occasionally twitched on the surface, this fly would call up trout that seldom saw the light of day.

As we left Jack to himself, we paused to observe his technique. He was a quick study, getting twenty to thirty feet of line out with passable grace. When that first mega-brookie smashed the fly he was sure to miss it, but he would catch on in a strike or two.

That night, as always, the cedar waxwings were the first to know. Gathered in kettles of six to eight, they swooped at the pond's surface snatching the unwitting mayflies before they became airborne. As the hatch intensified to full crescendo, the waxwings could no longer keep up and a surplus of may-flies began to accumulate on the surface. Oh, Christmas morning! Then came the trout!

One here. One there. Another. Another. It is an angler's finest hour, if it lasts an hour. Using our hex specials, we were intent on making the best of it. In a short time our veteran two-some had the first of a succession of fine fish on. After each one of us kept a fish for the fire, we were putting the rest back. We observed, however, that Jack seemed to be spending an inordinate amount of time tying-on and otherwise futzing with his flies. Come on, Jack, just stay with the hex. What's the problem?

Just as the light began to critically dwindle, Jack gave out a yell. "Hey! Come here! Quick! Big trouble! Get your asses over here! Quick!" We couldn't make out the details, but it was clear that he was not mortally wounded. Yet, there was a strange urgency in his tone. Maybe he had one on. Perhaps he just didn't know how to land it.

As we joined up and closed remaining distance, we could see that Jack had moved off the ledge onto flat ground. His line was slack.

"What's up, Jack?"

"Watch this," he said. Lifting one eyebrow, he pointed out on the water in the direction of his line and raised the rod. A small trout jumped in response. Then it jumped again. And again. Then, it uncannily rose into the air in a flutter and flew twenty feet to the left.

"I'll be a son-of-a-bitch. It's a bat!"

We couldn't believe our eyes. But there it was, irrevocably hooked.

Yes, a silly, stupid . . . *rabid* bat!

"Jack," I said with a straight face, "this happens all the time. Pull in the line so you can get at him. Then just grab the bat behind the head, like you would a snake, and work the fly out with these." I offered him my forceps.

"Quite routine," my other buddy chimed in, supporting the suggestion with an equally straight face.

Jack started to pull the bat in. We held our breath. When Jack had about fifteen or twenty feet of line left (plus nine feet of leader), he stopped taking up line and just backed up, dragging the bat onto the shore. As soon as the bat got on dry land, it fluttered chaotically, making pathetic two-foot saltations.

"Screw you guys. You're outta your friggin' gourds!" Jack responded belatedly but decisively.

Despite the misery the poor creature was clearly exhibiting, we all began to split a gut laughing at this unique situation. The laughter, however, was interrupted when the bat, with a single flapping vault, closed half of the thirty-foot distance between us and him. We scattered like flies before a horse's tail. In seconds we had put another fifty feet between us and him, leaving the offending rod right where Jack had dropped it.

By now it was almost dark, and we had to act while we could still see. We waited for a few minutes to see if the bat would move again. Nothing. "The hell with it," I said with resolve. I took out my knife, walked out to the rod, and cut the line, right at the reel.

Jack's borrowed line, that is to say my line, was a very expensive weight-forward. With one cut it became high-grade twine, temporarily stored on my old Pfleuger reel. Its shooting head and short taper was left on the beach.

As to the bat? Well, many a glass of Metaxa was raised in its honor that evening. The next morning, when we went back to look, he was gone. Also gone was the line remnant, the leader, and the seductive fly that was his undoing. Did he fly away, line and all? He surely would impress the hell out of his fellow bats with one wild fishing story. Or did he fall victim to some other predator that got its very first taste of fresh bat meat? These questions still seek answers.

As to Jack? Well, *that* was his swan song fishing trip. He still comes to Vermont to visit, usually to take a quick break while they're running at Saratoga. But now he calls ahead to make sure that no one has plans for an outing.

You know, he also claims to have turned an occasional dollar at the track by betting on horses with names like Salt n' Battery, Batter-Up, and Bat Boy.

Little Rock Pond

Hexagenia are huge, butterfly-sized mayflies that favor lakes and ponds with muddy bottoms. Local "hex" vary in color from green-tan to cream. You can see them on the surface of the water at incredible distances. Even in fading light, you can easily spot their pale forms at three or four hundred feet. As far as I'm concerned, that two- to three-minute time span, from when that hex nymph comes to the surface until it takes flight, provides the most exciting dry fly fishing there is to be had in Vermont. During a hatch, every trout big enough to drag one under gets involved. It is a feeding Mardi Gras.

Nowhere does this Mardi Gras make my pulse race harder than at Little Rock Pond in the town of Wallingford. Just shy of twenty acres in size and resting at an elevation of 1,854 feet on the flanks of the southern Green Mountains, its cool, very clear water and prolific crayfish population grow some of the most impressive brook trout left in the state. Brookies running ten to twelve inches are common. Larger fish are caught often enough to set my expectations high. My personal best from this pond is a fifteen incher.

The most common access to Little Rock Pond is a hike-in from the south, following the Long Trail. From U.S. Route 7 just east of Danby, visitors head east on the Mt. Tabor Road. As the road snakes steeply up into the mountains, it becomes U.S.F.S. Highway 10. In two miles or so, just before you cross the Black Branch, you will see a busy parking lot on the right. You're about to intersect the Long Trail and the Appalachian Trail—they are one and the same trail here. Little Rock Pond is a two-mile hike north. The trailhead is right across the road from the parking lot.

If you are unfamiliar with the Long Trail, you should know that with respect to the Appalachian Trail, the Long Trail has its own bragging rights. First off, even though it is only a fraction of the length of the AT, it is 265 miles long. That's a fair enough stretch for anybody's calf muscles. But even though the Long Trail is, in fact, short in comparison, it claims seniority over its younger and longer cousin. Created and protected by the Green Mountain Club, the Long Trail is North America's oldest long-distance hiking trail, opening to hiking traffic in about 1910. It served as both a model and an inspiration for the Appalachian Trail. And the Long Trail can dish up some nasty hauls. It seems that switchbacks—mercifully common in the Rocky Mountains—were completely unknown to those hearty, turn-of-the century easterners who laid out the Long Trail's route. I am happy to report, however, that the segment of trail near Little Rock Pond is easy. The two-mile jaunt from trailhead to Little Rock climbs only a few hundred feet. It is well maintained—one could even say manicured—with boardwalks in all the wet spots!

Because of its beauty, its location on the LT/AT, and its relatively easy access, do not expect solitude at the pond. It is one of the most heavily visited areas on the Long Trail. Camping at the pond is permitted in designated spots only. The Green Mountain Club maintains a caretaker here, a necessary and very welcome feature, given the circumstances. A fee is charged for overnight stays. It's well worth the expense to catch the very last moments of daylight and discover what Little Rock has to offer.

The fishing pressure is not at all in proportion to the heavy traffic that this place sees. I am amazed how very few of the hordes of people who visit and camp at this pond will fish. Most evenings I've had the pleasure of fishing the place all to myself. The locals come in the spring, fanning out along the massive rock outcrop that commands the west side of the pond. Most hike out before day's end. They do fine for a few weeks with fishing bait.

Most of my visits have been at the height of summer. By the time the 4th of July comes around—when the hex hatch usually starts—trout fishing is largely limited to the last hour or two of the day. The south end of the pond has been my hot spot. I first encountered the hex there, and in truth, I haven't been able to bring myself to try the north end of the pond, except in off-peak time. Hex can be a surprisingly local phenomenon on a pond. So far my desire to know what's going on at the north end of the pond has always been easily overpowered by my certain knowledge of those hex hatching in

Forked-Tail Hexagenia — Tail: two of dark cream cock hackle; Body: dyed fur mix of medium olive, yellow, and cream; Wing: bucktail; Hackle: dark cream cock hackle, wrapped parachute; Head: as body and finish with dark cream thread.

the fading summer light at the southern end. Some of the brookies that come up for them leave a wake like a beaver!

Casting from shore is difficult, and there are only a few places you can get a line out any distance. If you have the good fortune to own a fishing tube, pack it—this is exactly the kind of place it was meant to haunt.

Although there are a number of hex patterns commercially available, when it comes to producing strikes, I have found them to be no improvement on a Muddler Minnow. In #10 or larger, it will consistently take its share.

My preferred imitation is of my own device and employs a forked-tail and a parachute hackle. I favor cream colored hackles for the tails and the parachute. The latter is wrapped around a singular wing. For the wing I use a variety of material—the lightest colored tips of squirrel tail, cream dyed calf-tail, or light parts of the bucktail all work well. I use #10 - #6, 3x long hooks. On still water, the large hook, the parachute hackle on the single wing, and the forked tail work in concert to produce one of the most stable, true-cocking flies I've ever cast. This sucker sits out there like a little sailboat among the flotilla of little natural sailboats that constitute this most exciting of Vermont hatches. Give the sitting fly an occasional twitch and watch out!

Things That Go
Bump in the Water

For the fly fisherman the hour after sunset holds a special magic—the promise of rising trout. One evening in early spring, at the edge of a backwoods pond in Vermont's Northeast Kingdom, I was deeply in the grip of this magic.

My wife and I had packed in on the previous day to share a weekend. At that moment, however, she was getting little of my attention. My mind was on trout, and my eyes were on the water. I was on automatic pilot, scanning the expanse of the pond, then momentarily riveting on a few square feet of water where an insect or polliwog would break its placid surface, then resuming the scan.

Although the sun had set below our local horizon, it was still shining on the rest of the world, and the sky remained bright blue. The pond was glass slick. In the cool spring air a thin steam rose from its surface and sluggishly swirled. I saw no sign of trout.

Then all hell broke loose in the middle of the pond.

By the sheer size of its wake, I instantly took it to be a swimming deer or moose. It was only a fleeting thought, for this "creature" was not only too big to be a moose, it was moving at an uncanny—let me say *disturbing*—speed.

"It's the Champlain Monster! What the sweet bahjeezus is going on?" My wife put down the book she was reading, came to immediate attention to where I was pointing, and joined me in gawking at the most bizarre and unsettling sight that either of us had ever seen. If you think our mutual conclusion a bit rash, or even hysterical, let me describe in exact detail what we saw.

Five or six hundred feet away a creature undulated through the water at breakneck speed. It was at least twenty feet long, maybe thirty or more. It was difficult to judge as its entire body would never surface at one time. Instead, we saw a series of large humps heaving rapidly through the water. Two, three, or four of them appeared at a given time. Each hump was about three feet in length. As the creature swam, the humps would break the surface in an orchestrated, coordinated manner. It was exactly as some giant snake would swim, except that the waves of this thing's body were up-and-down, not side-to-side.

I couldn't believe this was happening. Of course I had casual exposure to the "Champ" legend, including one friend's firsthand account, which she told with embarrassing conviction. She was sure she had seen Lake Champlain's equivalent of the Loch Ness Monster. As to my own view, I had always been the most severe of skeptics. As I watched, however, my skepticism was evaporating by the millisecond. My senses were reporting that a nearly mobilehome-length sea serpent was frolicking across a backwoods pond that was probably about fifty feet deep.

Perhaps ten or fifteen seconds had passed since the creature first surfaced. My binoculars! I dropped my rod where I had been literally dancing in agitation and ran toward the tent for my field glasses.

More seconds passed. By the time I returned, trembling, with the glasses in hand, the leviathan had made its way a considerable distance down the pond. Focusing on it with the binoculars, everything looked exactly as I have described it, except now I could see the color and texture of the "humps." They were dark chocolate to black, slick and smooth as an eel.

As I peered through the lens, it appeared to slow, then in classic Champ fashion, reared its head from the water. At immediate impression, it presented a facial silhouette not unlike a brontosaurus, but smaller. *Much* smaller . . .

It was an otter! More precisely, a group of at least four, maybe five, otters whose head bobbing lasted only a few seconds before they regrouped and resumed their regimented mode of travel. One followed the other, alternately making low dives and surfacing in a very straight, very long formation.

I have seen otters many times and know that my secondary identification was one hundred percent accurate.

I was perhaps a little embarrassed with myself, so upon returning home, I thought I would try to make sense of what I had seen. My Audubon guide to mammals indicates that the size of otters range from thirty-five to more than fifty inches. Since they can also weigh up to thirty pounds, we are considering a pretty good-sized animal to begin with. For the sake of argument let's say we have a group of four otters, each about forty-four inches long. Since they are not likely to swim exactly tail to nose, let's allow three feet between them. The length of this resulting "creature" would be well over twenty feet long. Add another otter to the group, a little space in the queue for him to swim in, and we get a thirty-foot monster.

The character of their rhythmic, linear formation is something that can be observed in other animals. I am reminded of seeing pelicans flying in a undulating line, or the way schools of fish dart in unison. Geese, it is said, fly in a line to take advantage of the aerodynamic draft created; the lead bird cuts through the "unbroken" air, making it easier for those that follow.

Otter in Lake Champlain? You bet. They feed on fish, and I have seen them on several occasions in the Winooski River, right in the city of Winooski. If they are there, they are in the big lake for sure; it is one great fishery for them. Since they are powerful swimmers—anything that can catch a trout would have to be—it would not be unlikely to see them in the broad lake, even miles from shore.

Realizing that none of my speculation about "humped" sightings in Lake Champlain will abet the Vermont T-shirt and souvenir industry, I am nonetheless fully satisfied that Champ sightings are created by nothing more than a spirited group of otters enjoying an outing. Sighting such a group in the open water of the broad lake, where there are few references for scale and distance, would produce a convincing case for Champ to any spectator. Had my binoculars not allowed me to see the real nature of this most remarkable apparition, I would have become a zealous Champ convert, no doubt, scorning others as being so naive as to believe that his travels are restricted only to Lake Champlain.

Ducking At Duck

The trip started out quite routine . . . routine, like the last meal served to the condemned prisoner.

Since we had a late summer backpacking trip to Idaho's Big Horn Crags planned, four of us took it to mind to do a bit of a shakedown cruise. Our destination was among a cluster of backwoods ponds in the town of Sutton, Vermont. None of us had made a previous visit.

We would stuff those 4,500-cubic-inch packs as if we were going out for ten days, then take a roundabout hike into the pond for an overnight fish-in. The theory was to build up a little endurance for the Idaho jaunt.

As to where we would put our rods to use and our heads to the pillow, we decided on Duck Pond. To make for a longer hike, we would start from Big Wheeler Pond, about two miles north of Duck, and take the serpentine trail that was indicated on our maps. This would give us about an eight-mile round trip over the twenty-four-hour bivouac.

We arrived at Big Wheeler around noon. It was late July, sweltering hot and humid. In addition to what we would actually need, each of our packs was filled with enough ballast to weigh about seventy pounds. They felt murderously heavy as we shouldered them, locked the cars, and headed in. The rough trail snaked through a lush green forest with much open floor. The high emerald canopy was beautiful and provided just enough shade to spare us heat stroke.

This being the first "power hike" of the season for all of us, nobody was singing trail songs as we zig-zagged our way to Duck in the heat of a breezeless summer afternoon. It felt like we had done about ten miles when we dropped the packs at Blake Pond. Like French Legionnaires in a B-movie, we immediately stripped and plunged, screaming, into the pond. The cool water, a hefty snack, and about an hour's rest were enough to revive us for the last quarter mile to Duck Pond.

We put our burdens down in the large clearing at the south end of Duck Pond. Our horizon was a nice view of the leeward side of Mt. Hor on the horizon at the far end of the pond. Beautiful. We made camp and cooked a hasty supper on the MSR stoves. We were as wiped a bevy of sedentary forty-some-things as you can imagine.

It was pretty close to six o'clock when I strung up my rod and began fishing. Even with the encouragement of the ten-inch brookie I soon caught and released, I knew I was not going to make it to the magic fishing hour around sundown. An early crash and up with the birds, now that sounded like a plan. I was not at all alone in these ruminations—indeed, I was the only one who had bothered to put a rod together. It was not yet seven o'clock when we began to talk openly about hitting the sack. In minutes we were getting things in order to head for the bags.

Suddenly we heard what sounded like a lawnmower bawl-ing in the distance. The sound grew louder, then a beat-up VW Beetle sped into camp. With a hundred or more feet of clearing to select from, it parked abruptly fifteen feet from one of our pitched tents. It immediately disgorged two camp-ers—Leon and Roy.

Yes, they had the prominent tattoos—skulls, blood-dripping daggers, and old girlfriend's names that had resisted eradication—but they were congenial enough. They immediately came up to introduce themselves and check us out.

They assured us they personally had fished out the pond last May, warned us about the bears, and offered detailed directions on how we might drive our cars in the next time we came. They then proceeded to break into one of the two cases of beer they had brought along, offering us a six-pack with genuine hospitality. We declined politely.

Our thoughts about immediately bedding down had evaporated. Even if we could have overcome the embarrassment of going to bed at seven o'clock on a sunny July evening, the incessant banter and arguing in which the two were constantly engaged would have made sleep impossible. They argued about everything—how to pitch their tarp, where to build their fire, who owed who money for beer and gas, where the best place was to lay a bullet into a charging bear, and so on.

When all was said and done they pitched their tarp right off the VW, extending their territorial claim to within eight feet of our tents. We found this especially remarkable because the clearing was very large and offered several alternative sites. Although all of this was characterized by a completely affable demeanor, it was more disconcerting than flattering. Moments before, we had been blissfully tired, ready for bed and being serenaded by a chorus of thrush in a spectacular natural setting. The transformation was as profound and as instantaneous as switching channels on TV. Well, that's enough of PBS's Nature, let's watch the movie on Channel 11—"Freddy Krueger and his Minion Go Camping."

Then, the surreality absolutely blossomed as they began to build their fire. They made a beeline for an abandoned culvert and proceeded to break off two-and three-inch-thick slabs of this obsidian-like tar coating. In a very short time they had amassed fifty pounds of this stuff. They then threw about forty pounds of it into a hastily scraped fire ring, added a couple of pieces of wood as a garnish, and set the black mass ablaze. The resulting fire was an eerie preview of the oil field fires of the Gulf War. The thick black smoke billowed skyward as they broke out a gaggle of chicken parts and laid them on a grill they had brought along for the task.

Leon—the barbequemeister—barked directions at Roy as to how to precisely position the grill. In the end, the chicken lay in the exact plane where the Halloween orange flames gave birth to the dense inky fumes of the tar smoke. The four of us exchanged furtive glances and bit our lips near bloody.

The generosity of these two tattooed waifs can hardly be overstated. No sooner was the chicken warm than it was pulled from the fire. The dish looked very similar to Louisiana blackened cuisine, except these had an attractive rainbow shimmer when they caught the light just right. Select pieces of these semi-raw, ebony carcasses were offered to us. We declined and by now were appearing to be rather abstemious old farts to this devil-may-care duo.

As Leon and Roy worked through the chicken and beer, the adrenaline that their advent had stirred in us began to wear off. As the twelfth empty can of beer joined the others in the flaming tar pit, I was again realizing just how bushed I was. Glancing at the remaining thirty-six full cans, now amassed in Napoleonic formation at the water's lapping edge, and seeing the pile of extra batteries for the boom box radio that had by now emerged from the limitless bowels of the VW, I began to think that things could hardly be worse.

Quite simply, I was dead wrong.

More visitors.

With little warning to herald their coming, two pickup trucks pulled into the clearing. They were filled with laughing, drinking, shrieking, Frisbee-throwing, bandanna-dog-owning students from Lyndon State College—or so we guessed.

The new crowd was co-ed and numbered about a dozen or so. Everybody waved at everybody. Of course, because Leon and Roy camped right on top of us, the new arrivals thought we were all together and that Leon was our leader, because he never let up on barking orders, telling Roy what to do.

The newly arrived troupe branched out with the coordination of South American army ants and very quickly denuded the entire compound of any downed wood. Then out came the axes, hand saws, and even a chainsaw, as they continued to amass fuel for what was sure to be the mother of all bonfires.

As soon as Leon and Roy saw the chainsaw they became socially ignited. They struck up a conversation with the students and complimented them on their preparedness. Of course, Leon and Roy usually bring a chainsaw when they camp but since they were coming here, they knew there would be plenty of culvert tar and they wouldn't need much wood. The students returned the preparedness compliments by referencing the three dozen beers that were at-the-ready in the shallow water and expressing their own concerns that they might have to send one of the trucks back to the store.

We were in a state of mental collapse as we imagined what else the evening would hold in store for us. Was that a conga drum in the back of the truck?

Time passed. The college crowd eventually figured out that Leon and Roy were not out with us on a fathers-and-sons fishing trip. Once they had done that, the social fabric of the encampment quickly developed into "us" and "them." Leon and Roy abandoned the smoldering tar pit and took up seats at the bonfire near some of the women, hoping against hope that somehow the gods of love would favor them with a miracle.

As darkness began to gather and the bonfire spewed sparks twenty feet into the air, their talk turned once again to bear.

Then the guns came out. The college crowd bragged a .22 carbine, a 410 single-shot, and a small .22 revolver. Leon had a 12-gauge shotgun with a pistol grip and vented barrel. Roy had an army surplus .45. They were passing these freely around as the partiers slapped each other on the back and brandished the weapons toward the far edge of the clearing.

We were at our physical limits, and the coming of the night was all we needed. We gave them a good night wave and headed for the bags. We knew that there was going to be a few hours of rowdy drinking, but we felt bushed enough to hope for sleep, noise or no noise.

Again, dead wrong.

Apparently, we had been the parental authority figures in this encampment. So, as soon as we were tucked in and out of sight, the festivities intensified to bacchanalian proportions. Over the next hour or so, to a musical score of ear splitting heavy metal rock n' roll, the scene escalated from shotgunning beers to shotgunning shotguns.

If ever there was a horde of accidents waiting to happen, this assemblage was it. Here they were, completely plastered, passing around loaded guns, swilling additional mass quantities of beer, and shooting off rounds toward the other side of the lake. Any bears sneaking up on the bonfire from that end of the lake had to be deaf or suicidal, given the hail of gunfire that Leon et al were putting out in their direction.

At each report of a .22 our stomachs cramped with fear. When either the .410 or the 12-gauge went off, we would thrash into the air an inch or two off our sleeping pads, like cardiac patients being jolted with the electric paddles. We were literally getting hit in the face by each blast. Our geodesic dome tents were tautly pitched, and their coated ripstop skins produced enough tympanic action to actually blast air into our faces in concert with each round fired.

The occurrence of shots was completely unpredictable. Rapid volleys were followed by interminable minutes of waiting. We just lay there with knotted stomachs and funny-tasting mouths, re-running bloody movies of one kind or another in our minds. Every now and then one of us would mutter something about going out there, ripping one of the guns out of their hands, and keeping them all covered while the rest were disarmed. But each time the suggestion was made, it was thought better of, and we just cowered low. The waiting was the worst. KABOOM!

Sometime around two in the morning the last beer was drunk and the last cartridge was fired. They had run out of both. Leon and Roy retired to their tent. Being within ten feet of them, we had the full benefit of their anatomical descriptions of each of the women, along with one or two improbable reasons as to why they hadn't brought them to bed.

Around three a.m. we fell asleep, reasonably confident that we would live to see another day.

At seven in the morning this confidence was badly shaken as Leon and Roy made their departure. These boys defied belief. A scant four hours ago, drunker than skunks, they had crawled under their tarp and passed out. Now they were up and at 'em—still completely hammered, of course, but with places to go, people to see. They packed up their gear in less than fifteen minutes, hopped in the VW bug, and tried to start the car.

I sat up just in time to view the process through the drawstring screening of the tent's window. If I have neglected so far to mention the ten- to fifteen-degree slope that interposed the scant distance between our tent and the VW, it is because until that moment it seemed of little significance.

As the VW failed to start, rolling three feet at us in the venture, it became apparent that the Bug had no emergency brake—or worse, Roy just was too drunk to notice.

There we were, ground zero in the flight path of the VW. Another turn of the key and the car rolled toward us with its starter whining like a banshee. After four feet of accelerating roll, Roy hit the brakes and held the car fast.

Taking courage in the fact that Leon and Roy were out of ammunition, one of our party yelled out of the tent at them.

"No sweat, buddy," Leon yelled back, "Roy'll ge' the somnabitch next try."

Well, Leon was right. Roy did get it on the next try. He might have even had a couple feet to spare as the engine roared to life. Demonstrating consummate and clearly instinctive driving skill, he jammed on the brakes, instantaneously slammed it into reverse, and surged the car back up the incline, blasting the tent with sand and gravel.

The VW disappeared behind a cloud of noxious blue smoke and, along with Leon and Roy, was out of our lives. I remember nothing at all of the rest of the trip. I suppose that we beat it out of there as quickly as possible that morning, returning to our cars by the shortest route. We'd had all the "training" for our Idaho trip that we could stand.

You know, I cannot think of another place in Vermont from which I've taken a ten-inch brookie and not paid a return visit. Duck Pond will always remain the exception.

Holland Pond and Neighbors

The early Vermonters whose opinion held sway in the naming of the state's physical features showed a real sense of humor, if not outright perversity, when it came to designating our water bodies either a lake or a pond. Although most people would expect a pond to be smaller than a lake, those who were in charge seemed to have little regard for this convention. As a result, we have places like "Lake of the Clouds," a mere pothole of rainwater on the ridgeline of Vermont's highest mountain. You can literally spit across it when the wind is right—and it is often right. And then we have places like Holland Pond.

At a mile and a half from top to bottom and more than a half-mile across, Holland Pond hardly seems like a "pond" at all. And, for the record, it doesn't technically qualify as a pond. In fact, it fails on each of the parameters that most commonly define a water body to be a pond or not. Unlike a true pond, it does not have a uniform temperature distribution. On the contrary, with a maximum depth of nearly forty feet, it physically supports temperature stratification. Its shoreline is affected by wave action. And, even if sunlight can penetrate to its bottom throughout its extent—a fact about which I am not at all certain—it is rocky enough, in places, to thwart plant life. A true pond is supposed to have the ability to support plant life from shore to shore.

Holland Pond is a lake, but a rose by any other name would smell as sweet, and, for my taste, Holland is as sweet as they come.

For many years I restricted my attentions to the early season. Because of that, I missed out on one of the most regular hatches of hexagenia in the state . . . but I'll come back to that. Holland Pond has a lot more going for it than the fishing. In fact, if it is big fish that you want, you are better served by heading to Willoughby, Seymour, Echo, or any of a couple dozen other lakes. Although there are four-pound rainbows mounted on the walls of its lakeside camps, these are few and far between.

Holland Pond, in the town of Holland, sits a mile or so south of the Canadian border. It is situated at the western edge of one of Vermont's largest tracts of undeveloped land. The almost twenty miles of mountainous forest between here and the Connecticut River Valley is broken only by a spider web of logging roads and State Route 114, the latter being largely a vehicular bowling alley for moose.

The attraction of this area has always been its unspoiled and wild expanse. Much of the west side of Holland Pond is lined with summer camps. The east side of the lake, however, is part of the Bill Sladyk Wildlife Management Area. At nearly 10,000 acres, it is the largest such area in the state. Holland's surrounds include a few named lakes and ponds, as well as several unnamed beaver ponds and flowages.

It is rich with wildlife. Early in the spring you can look for bear tracks around its outlying ponds. There are deer, moose, grouse, and a variety of raptors. It is also the stronghold of the emblem of northern latitude water bodies—the loon. Even when their numbers were frighteningly low, their tremolos were heard in these parts. Nowadays the loons are coming back strong, and there are usually pairs on several of the water bodies in this area.

It was the promise of seeing moose that first led me to Holland's shores in the early '70s. At that time the Vermont moose population was restricted just about exclusively to the state's northeast corner. Their appearance here, then, was still enough of a novelty to impress the local denizens. On my very first visit, I hadn't walked a quarter mile along the trail that hugs Holland's northwestern shore when I was thrilled by my first sighting of moose tracks in Vermont soil. Later that day, fishing a small beaver dam in its upper watershed, I had a memorable encounter with a bull.

This moose had a rack the size of a living room couch and grazed along the edge of the impoundment. In fact, he had gnoshed his way on pond-bottom along several hundred feet of the water's edge, crossing from Canada to the United States in the process. The boundary is in general well defined by a series of obelisk markers and a forty-foot swath cut through the forest, technically termed the "boundary vista." I was successfully exploiting an international "no-man's water," where the beaver dam and impounded water blurred the exact location of the line. I'll go on record as saying that it was my studied impression that my feet—and, of course, my casts as well—were always on the U.S. side. If, however, an occasional Canadian fish chose to flee family and country in pursuit of my #14 Henryville Special (and many were doing just that), well, there was no extradition for them. The very best of them were going to the pan.

The moose, which I had also been watching for the better part of a half-hour, worked its way to within a hundred feet of where I was casting dry flies to these exceptionally hungry eight-inch brookies. As you might imagine, I wasn't willing to give ground immediately. When he got close enough to make me begin to feel uncomfortable, however, I decided to emphasize my presence. I took off my hat and began to sing what has become my standard for a moose encounter, set to the tune of "Hello Dolly": "Well Hello, Moosey / It's sure swell, Moosey / It's so nice to have you . . ." The huge bull pawed the ground and lowered his head. I had a moment of panic as he advanced a few feet. I immediately stepped in over my hip boots and soon was nearly up to mid-calf in mucky pond bottom—the same stuff this guy had been eating! I remember thinking that, when

71

he ultimately stomped my ass, the muck would afford me a little cushion, perhaps giving me an edge on surviving the trouncing. As it was, these thoughts, along with my wet-legged retreat, proved to be unnecessary. The bull trotted off into a dense stand of black spruce. Moving away from me, in apparent slow motion, his dark shape coursed through the dark forest, knocking aside or leveling all vegetation that challenged his path.

Holland Pond has always done okay by me. For a number of years I had such good luck taking brookies and small rainbows from its northern end that I ignored the southern two-thirds entirely. (Those who motor around might sample several locations at dusk, but for those of us who paddle, row, or walk the shore, a choice must be made as to where to fish during that last hour of light.) The northern end of the pond holds several attractions for me. It has a couple of significant inlets, one draining Beaver Pond and the other getting its water from Line, Round, and Turtle ponds. Its shoreline drops off relatively quickly to twenty or more feet of water. In places its bottom is strewn with large rocks, providing a structure-rich environment for trout. It has another important feature: sheltered coves that provide hope for dry fly fishing even when there's a fair chop on the water.

Flies? Below the surface, I've done well with Wooly Worms, Picket Pins, and a little charmer of a nymph that can be tied at a rate of a dozen or more an hour. (See "No Name Nymph" below.) Of course, a Gray Ghost trolled or cast will do the trick. Hornbergs, fished dry or wet, will do it, too. For dry flies, Blue-Winged Olives #16 - #18, March Browns #10, Black Gnat Parachutes #16, Hendricksons #12, and caddis in all sizes have done well. Then there are the hex.

From the beginning of July and on into August the hex hatch is the featured event in this part of the world and, until 1995, I didn't have a clue that it was happening. The lake's southern end holds a wide expanse of shallow water. Here the water is ten feet deep or less and weedy. Very early in my history of fishing Holland Pond, a friend and I were reduced to trolling for strikes. The only fish of that day was a scrawny nine-inch pickerel that we took on a Gray Ghost while trolling the southern shallows. It was a put-off for me and reinforced my habit of stalking only the northern end.

Several years ago, though, I managed to engineer our family vacation at Holland Pond. We took a cottage on the lake's southern shore for the third week of July. I was pleased to have arranged to have my family in one of my favorite fishing haunts for a whole week, but fishing was not the top priority. Enjoying the time with my family held my fishing urges in check until the sun drew low on the horizon. In truth, it was relatively easy to concentrate on family matters for nearly the entire day. The heat and sunny skies were relentless. Water skiers and towed tubers plied the bright waters. Other gasoline-burning yahoos were constantly running around the lake's perimeter in overpowered boats, exploring every nook and cranny at forty miles an hour.

Fishing in these conditions held little attraction for me. The days would be given over to swimming and nature walks, picnics and relaxation. Taking solace in the fact that the lake would be too warm for my surface tactics anyway, I had bargained in my own mind for an hour or so of fishing at the close of each day, but I did not expect much of it.

Since a boat and a motor came with the cottage rental, my game plan was to buzz up to the inlet from Beaver Pond and fish my usual spots. On the first day, Fate, in the form of a failed motor, intervened, and there I was at 8 p.m. in the shallow, weedy part of the lake. I was not very optimistic about the fishing prospects for this overall trip anyhow. Now, with the water overly warm and my assessment of the fishing potential diminished by the restrictive geography and shallow water with which I was presented, I could have given up. But pessimism be damned—I was going to fish anyway.

Devotion is sometimes rewarded. In retrospect, the salient feature about this part of the lake was *not* that it would kick up a pickerel from time to time, but rather that my immediate vicinity, by virtue of its immense expanse of muddy lake bottom, is one of the best hexagenia breeding grounds in the state! As the air cooled and the light faded, those giant mayflies emerged. In the languid, damp air of the July evening, they lingered on the surface waiting for their wings to dry. As they did, scores of fat rainbows came out of the woodwork and feasted. The hex were like a flotilla of Lilliputian sailboats, unaware that members of their regatta were being methodically picked off by sea-monster rainbows. The rally continued into the black of night.

As for myself, I tied on one of my hex parachutes and was in business with these foot-long trout until I could no longer see and striking at the sound of their rises became useless because there were so many trout rising. These fish were among the healthiest looking specimens that I've ever seen—fat, firm, and spunky.

What a week! Every night at 8 p.m. I had an appointment with the rainbows of Holland Pond. Every night, it ran like British rail. I showed, the hex showed, and the rainbows showed—all on time, and all the players doing just what we were supposed to do. Since that fateful week, I have placed Holland on my dance card for July as well as May.

Like Jupiter and its moons, Holland has its satellite ponds. If you can drag yourself away from the fish at Holland and explore its headwaters, you will find a remote piece of fishing real estate that, somewhat ironically, is one of my favorite places—Beaver Pond. I have camped on Beaver Pond for the last twenty-five years, throwing down a tent for at least a couple of nights in each of those twenty-five fishing seasons. (I've also slept a couple of frigid winter nights there, right out on the ice.) Although I've seen a thirteen-inch brookie taken out of here, I don't think I've personally caught twenty-five brookies during the span of time I've fished, and none of them are worth an individual mention. Perhaps the otters I've seen fairly regularly keep their numbers down. Despite my lack of angling success, I keep coming back. I come for the loons, the moose, the otter, the grouse, the great blue herons, the deer, the early spring osprey, the secret fields of lady slippers, and the chance to spend some time alone. Besides, Beaver Pond is forty acres large and eighty feet deep. It must hold some big ol' soaker of a square-tail with whom I have an appointment at a date as yet unknown.

Round Pond, another of Holland's satellites, used to have some of the best brook trout fishing in the state. In fact, aside from a handful of noteworthy brookies that I've taken individually in other places, Round Pond gave me my very best single day of brook trout fishing *ever*—including even my few trips to Quebec. Twenty years ago, this pond was serving up foot-long squaretails with such regularity that it seemed absolutely uncanny. And it was.

It turns out that the state of Vermont was maintaining those Round Pond trout by force of will and an extremely generous stocking policy. Once everyone sobered up (certainly by the mid-'80s), the pond was given over to its natural state as a warm water fishery. The brookies went away. It is still a great place to put it down for a day or two. It is centrally located and has a sturdy, dry lean-to. Surprisingly, it is in the winter season this place sees the most traffic. This area has some of Vermont's most popular snowmobile trails and, as a result, winter sees a steady parade of guests at the Round Pond lean-to. In the trout season, it is the opposite. I don't believe I've seen anyone in my short visits there for the last six or seven years.

Except for the beaver dams, the balance of the standing water in this area has not been kind to me. Duck Pond has never produced a trout for me but is a hot spot for moose and other wildlife. For the mere smattering of attention that I've given it, Turtle Pond has also failed me. As of this writing, I haven't visited it in five years, at which time I was told that the state was going to drop in some fingerling brookies. Although shore fishing with flies is limited on all the ponds in this area, Turtle Pond is edged in many places by bog and dead standing timber and is a good place to fish with a tube. (Note to self: Buy float tube.) The best trail from Holland Pond starts at the east end of "Turtle Cove," just north of the inlet. I've contemplated slogging a canoe, African Queen-style, up the inlet, but the fishing elsewhere is a known quantity and, in the face of the many defeats on Turtle, constantly wins over these exploratory instincts. If you've got a good pair of legs and don't care about trout fishing, Halfway Pond beckons. It's pretty enough, but it has been given over to pickerel and other coarse fish. Line Pond, which is more like a glorified beaver dam, has yet to show me a fish, but every few years I'll make the foray there, hoping that the Canadians have dropped in some beauties that have chosen to migrate to its southern end.

At times when fishing is off in Holland and Beaver (the latter, nearly always), the beaver dams in the area may hold the key to success. There are some on the inlet brook to Beaver that will usually yield some small brookies, and I've hit some larger fish (eight-inchers) in the fresh dams that occasionally pop up between Line and Turtle.

Fish or no fish, this area has captured my heart, and should a psychologist ever say "Holland" to me in a free association test, windmills and wooden shoes are not what would come to mind!

The "No Name Nymph" is a favorite wet fly that has done well on Holland Pond, as well as lots of other still water, and is extremely simple to tie. Start with a gold tag at the bend of a #12 or #14 hook and tie in a strand of fine gold wire. Lay down a body of medium olive dubbed fur right to the back of the head. Wrap the hackle forward, palmer-style, tie it down, then wrap the gold wire forward to secure your work. Whip finish the head and clip the hackle short.

No Name Nymph–Tail: gold tag; Body: dyed fur, medium olive, wrapped gold wire; Hackle: brown hen hackle wrapped palmer and clipped; Head: medium olive thread.

My Fishing Rods

With a fidelity that is now reflected in my marriage, I have always been a one-rod fisherman. I remember every one.

The first rod that I used was a despicable steel baitcaster. I was eight years old, and I received it—on loan—for my first fishing trip. As my father was also a one-rod man, his fishing friend had put together a makeshift outfit, which consisted of the five-foot metal rod (more suitable to fencing than fishing, as I recall it) and a plundered Pfleuger fly reel, half filled with a "well-seasoned" fly line. I was not at all impressed. It hardly compared to those shiny, bamboo, eight- and nine-foot Montagues that the men used. Although it was apparent that the real trout rods were nearly twice as long as the instrument they were giving me, I accepted it without question. Like a grateful hound, I was just plain nuts to go trout fishing. I got a couple of seasons out of this mini-utility pole and, in fact, managed to worm in a few trout. When I was through with it, the rod—along with the reel and even more seasoned line—was reclaimed by its owner. In the end, I was appreciative for its use.

My next rod was a eight-foot fiberglass Shakespeare. It was as white as Hopalong Cassidy's horse, with yellow wrappings on the guides. It sported a Pfleuger Medalist reel and a level floating line. Finally, a real fly rod. No hand-me-down, either. I was unique among my childhood peers in using a fly rod. All of my friends who fished used spinning gear. Let me hasten to point out that the fact that it was a fly rod had nothing to do with any intention to fish flies. It was not until the following season that I made that connection. During my formative years as a trout fisherman my standard m.o. was garden hackle, "found bait," or, best of all, garden hackle on a #6 or #8 Eagle Claw spinner. I'm sure if I went back to that technique I'd catch more and bigger fish. By the time I was in college, though, I was fishing with flies and still fishing the Shakespeare. It finally fell victim, as many do, to an over-sprung screen door at a Quebec fishing camp. In retrospect, I'd say it had an action that approximated that of an industrial broom.

The glass Phillipson 7½-foot for a 6 wt. came in 1971. It was the very first fly rod that I selected for myself. It had a nice, wimpy, so-called "wet fly" action, but not much backbone. Its slow action was really sweet for landing a dry fly with a hush. I loved it dearly and fished a few memorable seasons with it. But, unlike all my other rods, I cannot account for its ultimate fate. Whether it was put away somewhere and forgotten, given away, broken, or loaned is of no consequence. Relatively early in its career, the Phillipson was eclipsed by the gift of an Orvis.

The Orvis rod was probably the very best result of an otherwise mutually disastrous long-term relationship with a woman. She named a jointly held Siamese cat Trout as a way of deriding my enthusiasm for the sport. She loved to roll the R's when she said his name. Oh well, I have a laundry list of abuses at her hand, but, I'll say this in her favor, she knew how to make a guy happy on his birthday. On mine, she completely blew me away by giving me the finest fishing outfit I could have possibly conceived. Its core was a bamboo rod, a 7½-foot Battenkill for a 6 wt. line. It had *two* tips. I couldn't believe it. There were surgeons, dentists, and lawyers who would envy such a rod. It was way out of my social class. Hell, sometimes I barely had enough money to put gas in the car. Such a sweet thing . . . the rod, that is. It had a lot stiffer action than the glass Phillipson, but it also had a delicacy. I fished with it for a decade on everything from alder-choked brooks to windswept lakes above treeline. It took its knocks. I even got a snooty letter of reprimand from Orvis once for not drying it off before putting it back in its case. Its handle stunk to high heaven from trout snot and mildew, like every rod that I've owned. So, when I sent it to Orvis in Manchester for one of its biannual reconditionings, it evidently caused quite a stir among the workers. I, of course, penned a letter back telling them in no uncertain terms that the rod was mine to disrespect if I wanted to, and to otherwise piss off. In truth, I more than respected it. To my mind, it was the ultimate fishing instrument. If, at the time, I still aspired to becoming a "Samson" among trout fishermen, this would be the jawbone of my choosing. So much for vanities. I never slayed as many trout. One day, in haste to return a borrowed car, I drove off, leaving the broken down Battenkill on the trunk. It probably lay there for a while, right in a pull-off at Hollow Brook in Hinesburg. I think I might have made a mistake by phoning the state police about it. I never saw it again. The remaining butt-less tip was just a taunt in my closet, so I gave it away. Anyhow, it was time for a change. The world of graphite had come, and I embraced it.

I did make an earnest effort to find a rod for under a hundred bucks. I found a Cortland, eight foot for 5 wt. I tried it for about a month. It was a club. Snooty letter notwithstanding, I found myself coming back to Orvis, for they had spoiled me forever.

I settled on a 7' 9" Far and Fine for a 5 wt., and it pulled better than a decade of hard fishing. It had yet more backbone compared to the Battenkill and added considerably to my range. It was enchantingly light and a pleasure to cast. I went through a couple of tips on it. The second new tip began rotating. Waxing the male ferrule helped for a couple of years. Ultimately I found myself draping blades of grass over it to add substance to its diminishing diameter and counterbalance the steady erosion of graphite that occurs each time you take it down or put it together. It finally came to the point when I had to give up on it. One opening day, with the Far and Fine staying at home, I took after Lamoille River salmon with the Cortland. Bad mistake. Its cost? A bad case of "casting elbow," about twenty therapy sessions, and almost two months of no fishing. To those who suggested that I learn to fish with my other arm, I say that there are certain activities for which ambidexterity does not apply.

While in therapy (physical therapy, that is) I sent the Far and Fine back to Orvis. I really didn't think much could be done, and I was right. I had no complaints. I made it clear that I understood that it was just plain worn out. A natural death. I loved the rod. I had beat on it more than any rod ever deserved. I fished with it for a dozen years. No complaints. It had earned its current state of being. I wanted absolutely no consideration. But if you can fix it, how much? They said it was beyond hope. Then, bless 'em, they offered me a hundred bucks for it! I reviewed all of the above statements of satisfaction again and asked, "And you still want to give me a hundred bucks credit?" They said "No, a hundred dollars cash." I said, "Send me the check." When it came, I spent the hundred bucks, and then some, on my current rod, a 9-foot for 6 wt. Western, from Orvis's Rocky Mountain Series. It is more suited to lake and pond fishing than anything I've previously owned but can still offer delicacy on the stream, if you're careful.

All said and done, I think that there is little in the way of extraordinary in the history of my own rods, except that I've surprised myself in realizing that I remember them, when much else is forgotten. Perhaps I'll inspire your own inventory.

I have now found myself with a real preference for the longer rod. As for bamboo, I'll leave it to the collectors and those with money to burn. Despite its aesthetic qualities and unsurpassed delicacy, it can't take the abuse as well as the graphite and will never have the power. In the end, you pick a rod that will keep you happy. It is, after all, a magic wand that can vanquish all but life's grimmest heartaches. Remember the maxim expressed in the popular song: "If you can't be with the one you love, love the one you're with."

Getting Chummy

One of my favored stretches of fishing water was a mile-long reach of the Lamoille a mile or two upstream from where the Green River issues its cool water into the mainstem. I always shared the trip to this place with a particular friend. An old iron bridge spanned the river here, about a half mile south of Route 15, and was the jumping off point for our many forays. My steady fishing partner and I would take turns allocating the upstream and downstream sections of water to each other. It seemed to make little difference; the fishing was good either way.

One summer morning, however, the trout were sulking. The sunshine was brilliant and the temperature climbed rapidly throughout the morning hours, leaving us fishless, flushed, and sweaty. We rendezvoused at the metal bridge to eat our lunch and plot the afternoon's strategy. The bridge itself looked as if it had been built from a giant Erector Set, all raw function with no thought to appearance. The rust-proofing paint that coated it a dull red added only the smallest note of cheer. I'd never seen any car or, more likely, any tractor cross it, so we gave little thought to having our lunch right at the middle of its span.

As we ate our ham and cheese sandwiches, staring absently into the slow shaded run immediately under the bridge's upstream side, we noted four fat rainbows slowly swishing their tails to hold their position in the gentle but relentless current. They were spaced a couple of feet apart, and, in the clear water of a midsummer dry spell, offered us an opportunity to observe them clearly. These were indolent brutes who seemed interested in absolutely nothing above the level of basic respiration, which, as far as we were concerned, represented the state of all the trout in this part of the river. With slow, metronomic movements of their tails, these trout held like compass needles in the steady current.

A chance crumb of Cabot cheese, falling streamward from our hungry attack on the sandwiches, offered inspiration. Oh, it was wrong to do, I know. And we only justified it by the dubious premise that a trout returned is *not* a trout jacked. Cheese, of course, has a long history as an angling ploy, but we'll not go there now. Let me just say that the game plan was to chum these sleepy trout out of their summer lethargy and catch one.

Although neither of us had ever had any experience at this before (nor since, speaking at least for myself), the technique evolved instantly, as it seemed to suggest itself. As it proved out, it was also surefire.

We proceeded to roll pea-sized balls of the cheese, lobbed them upstream of the rainbows, and let them drift by. The trout held like Buckingham Palace guards, looking neither right or left, as the little white balls of cheese bounced by them at a regular pace. Then, when we were nearly halfway through throwing away the cheese part of our sandwiches, one of the rainbows broke ranks, drifted three inches to the left, and swallowed the cheese.

This trout returned to station for only a few moments, then it again broke ranks and drifted six inches to the left to gobble up another cheese offering. After two or three other successful feedings like this, the first trout was joined in the feed by one of its companions. From there things escalated quickly. Suffice it to say that in less than fifteen minutes we had frittered away nearly every last bit of cheese in both of our sandwiches, and there were four foot-long rainbows in a feeding frenzy, zipping this way and that in the stream—up to ten feet!—for a little piece of cheese.

With my knife I shaved all of the dressing off a #18 Quill Gordon (grudgingly calculating that it had taken me about twenty minutes to make the damn thing) and buried the bare hook in a ball of cheese of the exact size that we had been feeding them. I walked down to the river, and with expert guidance from my buddy who remained on the bridge . . . well, you know the outcome, and there is no glory in reporting on the fight. The very first fish that saw the proffered cheese ball float by took it like a kid takes a hot dog at the circus. It got itself a three-minute workout and was quickly back in the river with the other three trout, benefiting from our solemn resolve not to actually take the fish by such a low method.

As to the fish, the one we accosted went somewhere to sulk while the other three paced the run methodically, looking for more of the Cabot. We broke down the rods and drove back to Burlington, wearing broad smiles and carrying the secret of our enterprise in our blackened hearts.

The Oh-What-the-Hell Cast

To see the Seymour River as it flows north through Underhill, one could quite easily write it off as the domain of small trout. I want to dispel that notion right now and also add a little lesson in casting.

One fine May evening I zoomed up to the Seymour and parked the car in the swimming hole pull-off, about a mile upstream of Pleasant Valley. (Don't blink—this is more of a place-name than a place.) I never fish the swimming hole—which, come to think of it, could be a mistake—but always start in a hundred yards upstream or down. I hiked upstream to where the brook cuts into a rocky meadow. It is only eight or ten feet wide at the most.

The water was in great shape, maybe even a little on the low side, and running at optimum temperature. Evidently in a whimsical kind of mood, I tied on a stonefly nymph that was so grotesquely large that the 4X tippet, a residue of another night's fishing with smaller flies, seemed as gossamer. As I approached the stream I saw the jagged stump of a foot-wide tree. It rose about a foot and a half above the ground and was the prime agent in holding together the steep, undercut meadow bank. The stump itself was guarded by a narrow phalanx of five-foot-high bushes. These almost, but not quite, blocked my view of a nice deep run that was sure to hold a trout.

I was standing about fifteen feet from the edge of the bank. Continuing in this whimsical frame of mind, it became instantly apparent to me that a cast over the stump, and its attendant bushes, would give me perfect cover, perfect placement in the brook, and a grand view of the whole playing field. Of course, the only drawback was what to do if I should actually get a trout on the line. My line would come to rest right in the bushes, and I would have to fight any fish I hooked with my line running right through this growth. I thought, why not? If worse came to worse, I'd just horse it up and over the bushes.

I unhooked the stonefly from my rod's eyelet and falsecast out enough line to plop my offering and four feet of slack line—enough to impart some dead-drift time to the fly—right in the slot at the top of the run.

The stonefly landed invisibly in the last bit of whitewater, just above the head of the run and the deepest part of the hole. Given the size of my fly and the properties of polarized sunglasses, it was easy to pick it up as it entered the run and tumbled downstream. It dead-drifted a few feet without incident, but, as the rushing water ate up my slack and the stonefly began its short swing toward the end of my straightening line, a dark shape torpedoed from under my bank and made for the fly.

At first instant I didn't even connect the two events. The trout, in fact, was so big that I thought I had spooked some animal (like an albino mink!), and it was just high-tailing it away from me. By the time he nailed the stonefly, about two seconds after take-off, the mental pieces of this unfolding drama had all fallen together, and I recognized the attacker as a brown trout. I was shocked by the sheer size of this fish, which was not only completely out of the realm of my experience with Vermont trout in general, but was totally inappropriate to the size of this stream.

Regrettably, since "horsing" this soaker of a brown up and over the bushes was not going to be a successful tactic, I cannot say with certainty just how big he was. In the water (always an underestimate) he looked all of twenty-four inches.

As soon as I raised the rod and set the hook, the outcome was ordained. I made a gallant and successful attempt at getting my line out of the tangle of growth that held it. I fully extended my arm, pointing to twelve-o'clock high heaven and holding it rigid. The lower half of my body hobbled down to the stream under automatic pilot, as my eyes never left the trout. Just as I got into position streamside, he stopped fooling around, snapped the tippet without hesitation, and headed zig-zag downstream for Cambridge.

The ensuing two weeks nearly cost my marriage and sent stock in Mobil gasoline soaring. I haunted the banks of the Seymour every evening until I could no longer see what I was doing. The brown never showed again, even though I spent hours untangling my flies from those five-foot-high bushes.

Regarding my decision to make an absurd cast from a totally indefensible position, well, I have since added it to my quiver of trout tricks. It has unearthed at least one other monster brown for me, though with the same net result as above. It's better to have loved and lost, I think, than never to have loved at all.

The Lamoille River

The Lamoille River offers such fine fishing that it's surprising its reputation remains so local. From Hackensack to San Diego, every flatlander who waves a flyrod has heard about the Batten Kill. The Batten Kill is a river with a legendary reputation. But that's just because a select bunch of nineteenth-century New York writers apparently never had the fortitude to travel north to Fairfax, Jeffersonville, or Hardwick. Yes, the Batten Kill has big wild browns, but in many places its ambiance is lacking. Compared to the Lamoille River, the Batten Kill is an overrated, slippery-footed, tube-toting, canoe-infested, and tweed-promenading stretch of water. Moreover, to take full advantage of it you have to invest in a New York license. Vermont hosts only the first twenty-five miles of the Batten Kill, after which it drains the Empire State. For my money the Lamoille River is the place to come. With just a few exceptions, its eighty-five-mile length is a well-kept secret.

From its headwaters to its mouth the Lamoille is trout water. Far upstream, around Greensboro, it has first-rate brook trout fishing. From Hardwick to the Petersen Dam in Milton, it is peppered with lunker browns and rainbows large enough to impress. The fish below Cadys Falls will rival that of any stream with a national reputation. Downstream of the Petersen Dam, the word has spread about the mid-fall salmon runs, and now you're likely to meet nearly as many non-resident licenses there as local ones. This stretch also has an early-October run of steelhead that has attracted less attention.

The Lamoille downstream from Cambridge has always been kind to me. It gets much of my current attention because it is close at hand, about a half-hour's drive away. But it also offers the kind of fishing that is worth a hundred miles of driving. For many years a small cadre of friends and I fished a half-mile stretch that offered just phenomenal fishing for rainbows. We called it "T-H-E Spot." It is still a strictly kept secret now, twenty-five years after the flood of '73 wiped it out.

A few years ago, the state set aside a stretch of water that offers a nearly satisfactory re-creation of those bygone days. Today, from the Fairfax Dam downstream to the Route 104 bridge in Fairfax, the Lamoille River is managed for large trout. Lately it has provided great entertainment with browns that run thirteen to eighteen inches, but the specifics depend on what the state's been dropping in.

By report, the hottest fishing has been below the dam but, as you might expect, you can count on an abundance of company. For my taste, there is plenty of good fishing to be had in the stretch of water that runs downstream to Fairfax. Although there are times when I share a run of water with a stranger or two, most of the time I've got a generous piece of water all to myself. In a tradition with a thirty-year history, I nearly always fish this stretch with a dry fly.

Now, I already know a certain number of fishing folk are put off by the idea of catching stockers. Perhaps they have not experienced as much defeat at their hands as have I. For me, there is still honor in it. I can't attest for the experiences of the meat-n'-metal anglers, but taking stocked trout with a dry fly can offer as challenging an angling environment as any fishing. Sure, there are times when the stocked trout will seem to hammer just about anything thrown their way, but the same can be said of wild trout The stockers may succumb to a certain exuberance in the first week or so, but they quickly settle down. By season's end, I challenge any trout psychologist to demonstrate a difference worth mentioning between the past spring's drop-ins and trout that hatched out years before in the river. I've been as shut out by rising stockers as I have by those native-reared trout that have several seasons under their belts.

Whether fishing for the hard-to-please natives or gullible stockers, my most successful fly in this stretch of the Lamoille has been the caddis.

As far as store-bought flies are concerned, the Henryville Special (#14 - #16) and Western-style elk-hair caddis (#12 - #18) give a consistently good accounting of themselves. The elk-hair caddis that work best are in light-tan to cream. At those times when rising trout will not take the dry, I have turned the trick by going to a Pheasant Tail. This sparsely dressed nymph, in sizes #12 - #14, is a traditional pattern, and there are good reasons for the tradition.

I'd like to introduce you to my personal favorite fly—the forked-tail caddis. This fly not only produces well on this stretch of water, it can work anywhere, even with big, hard-to-fool trout. I think the secret of the forked-tail caddis is its crisp silhouette and its high-floating stance. The "forked tail" acts like an outrigger to keep the fly in proper orientation. Even if the trout aren't actively feeding on caddis, this offering looks so-o-o-o damn bug-like that I think it enrages the fish into an instinctive attack.

You begin tying the fly at its tail, which is actually two tails. Each is made of a pinch or two of shiny, stiff, and web-free neck hackles. The tail hackle length should be about equal to hook length. I most often select from a ginger or natural cream neck. One of the key elements in tying the tails is to tie each pinch of hackles to the shank at an angle away from the standard plane of a fly's tail. One tail points out to the left, the other to the right, at thirty to forty-five degrees off center. They are tied on, one side at a time. With a little practice, you can get the hang of wrapping the thread in X-wraps around the hackles to position them permanently away from the butt of the hook.

My preferred body material is natural fur from a hare's mask or tan-to-very-light caribou fur, spun around the shank and clipped to shape. In the latter case, I clip the top very close to the shank while leaving a more generous body on its sides and underbelly. This allows the "down" wing of the caddis to lie relatively flat on the top, and, in turn, helps to properly cock the fly when it lands.

For the wing of this irresistible little morsel, I prefer using a mottled light brown turkey quill. Now, traditional quill wings are notoriously finicky to tie and, even done properly, don't offer much in the wear-and-tear department. I solved both problems when "seam sealant" (for backpacking tents and outdoor clothing) hit the market. Applied to a wing quill, it's nothing short of miraculous. Give a quill a brush stroke or two, allow twenty minutes to an hour of drying, and the sealant transmutes the delicate structure of the quill's interlocking fibers to the consistency of flexible vinyl.

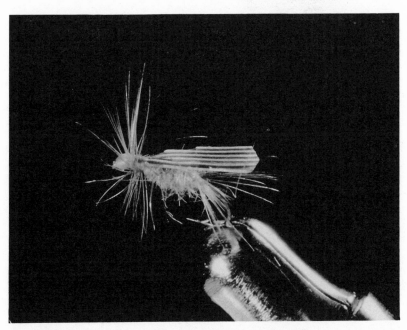

Forked-tail caddis — Tail: two of cream cock hackle; Body: lighter fur from a hare's mask; Wing: "seam sealed" turkey quill; Hackle: cram cock hackle; Head: cream thread.

I coat an entire quill at a time. There is perceptible shrinkage. Once the sealant has set, forget about peeling apart the quill along a fiber seam. It tears unsightly. Instead, you literally cut the wing right out of the side of the quill with scissors, to the exact shape and length you want.

I prefer to tie the tip side of the quills to the hook to take advantage of the natural narrowing of the material. I cut the "quill sheet" wide enough to cover the top.

Hold the wing in place over the fly. It will tie on as easily as anything you ever put to a hook. I tie the wing on, working back down the hook a little to assure a tight hold. The wing should be long enough to extend slightly beyond the bend of the hook.

Finish off like a standard dry fly by wrapping a couple of ginger/cream hackles forward to the head and whip finish.

Short Lines

The First Cast

The first cast over "virginal" water is key. We can all recount the number of times a really big fish has hit on that first cast, only to escape the hook through inattention. In fact, the number of times that happens is just about equal to the number of times that the brute will refuse to show himself again. The first cast should be well planned out. If there is a big trout there, it will have first claim on anything coming its way. After a couple of hours fishing with no signs of life, it is difficult not to drift. Those who execute that first cast in good shape and remain attentive will reap the benefits.

Keeping It in Perspective

Are you an "outie" or an "innie"? No, I am not talking belly buttons here. For many years I puzzled over which is the best way to tie on a fly—especially a dry fly—that has a turned-down eyelet on its hook. Some fisher folk have argued that the leader should be threaded through the hook's eyelet from the backside, sort of from the inside out. It has also seemed that an equal number of anglers hold that the leader is best threaded through from the front side of the eyelet. Oddly, I have heard both sides swear that their chosen method makes the fly cock correctly and float high on the water. I have spent months, even entire seasons, resolutely and consistently trying one way, only to have second thoughts and go over to the other method with as much devotion and without seeing any perceptible difference in results. In fact, more than a decade ago, I came to the conclusion that the issue had about as much weight as questioning on which side you should break an egg. Now, after forty years of throwing flies at fish, I have come to a final resolution of the debate: you thread the fly's eyelet through whichever side you can see.

Getting Skunked

Whoever coined the term "getting skunked" must have lived in an alternate universe. The etymology of the word, of course, refers to a skunk stealing your catch. The idea of a skunk crawling up your leg, opening your wicker creel, and relieving you of your catch is obviously absurd. And in broad daylight, even a cached trout stands a point-nine-nine-nine-nine chance of *not* succumbing to the predations of skunks, who almost always come out at night. When was the last time your trout were in jeopardy of skunks?

But getting marten-ed, well, that's entirely different.

Once, a marten—which is really an up-sized weasel—stole a trout clean away from me as I helplessly watched. I had worked myself along a shoreline of an extremely steep banked pond and was rewarded with a nice pan-sized fish. The going was so rough that I needed all four limbs to navigate. Since I had not packed in a creel, I temporarily stored the fish on a large rock near the shoreline. I then worked my way carefully along the shoreline, taking a good five minutes to move a mere twenty feet away.

When I first saw the marten, he was still some distance away. I yelled to my compadre, who was similarly challenging the local landscape to drop him into the pond, "Hey, check out the marten!"

We both then watched as he appeared, then disappeared, only to appear again, making his way directly at us, or so we thought. Each time he popped his head up, he looked us straight in the eye. Down he'd go, out of sight, then pop his head up again, sniffing the air and checking us out. Each time he did this little magician's act he came a little closer, and we oooh-ed and coo-ed at just how cute he was.

When he last popped his head up, he was holding my trout in his mouth. So much under his spell was I that I had forgotten all about the fish until he waved it in my face. He was only twenty feet away, as the crow flies (and maybe a crow would have had a chance), but he was every bit of five minutes away from me, and he seemed to know that fact, one hundred percent. He quickly pranced away with my fish, leaving me still looking for my supper.

On "Rod-Hours"

Some years back, a friend and I were humping down the trail to a favored pond, with hopes of catching the evening rise, when we encountered a sport who was headed back from our target pond.

"How's the fishing been?" we questioned him.

"Not that great," he replied. "I figure I went in around 5 a.m. Fished straight through 'til noon. Broke for lunch for about a half-hour, and then fished until about an hour ago. Let's see, it's four-thirty. That would have been around four that I quit . . . a half-hour to walk in this morning. So that's ten rod-hours. Let's see, I took only four fish. That's more than two rod-hours per fish. Let's call it two-and-a-quarter rod-hours per fish . . ."

A word to the true keepers of the fishing flame—*flee from people like this as if they were offering you fresh anthrax.*

Casting Tip

Called to the task, I have tried to teach casting many times. I am not a good teacher of this skill, and the combination of my failing efforts and the siren trout at hand will soon prompt me to part ways with the acolyte, usually with some admonition along the lines of, "Keep practicing." If you are, however, a fully trained caster of flies, I do have a single casting tip that will make a quantum difference in the ease and power of the backcast. Use a Wristlok™.

There may be other brands, and they may work as well, but the item that I encountered, and now swear by, is manufactured by the late Lee Wulff's company, Royal Wulff Products, Lew Beach, New York. The Wristlok consists of a wide wristband of leather that is wrapped around the wrist with a Velcro closure. A small leather sling hangs a couple of inches below the front of your wrist and accommodates the butt of the rod, "locking it to your wrist." Always, on the backcast, despite the firmest grip, the rod butt moves away from your wrist under the overwhelming mechanical leverage presented by the seven to nine feet of rod that is on the front of the action versus the few inches to a foot of rod that resides from the grip to the butt. The Wristlok limits the arc of the butt to within a couple of inches of your wrist, and all the energy that was lost to this movement now goes into powering your backcast.

Bank-kill

Someone once told me that you are not a true Vermonter until you've eaten roadkill. Well, I've done it. Once. It was a partridge that met its maker in Granby, shortly before I rounded the corner. I'll draw the line at "bank-kill," though, unlike the fellow I met from Vergennes, who claimed to have haunted the banks of Otter Creek tributaries in the days immediately after flashfloods. Bad idea.

Good Idea

Eating freshly caught trout is one good idea. Every time I serve it to my wife and daughter, who expect it regularly in season, it is announced with the phrase "Right now, there are kings and queens who are not eating as well as we are."

It would be a mean-spirited angler who did not recognize and mourn the value of the life he will take with a snap of the neck or a blow to the head. These fish are a wonderful little piece of the mysterious world that we share with them, and although I have much sympathy with the vegetarian point of view, I just don't subscribe to it.

Ideally, the fish should be eaten within the first few hours out of the stream. At their absolute freshest, a faint blue cast will be evident on the darker skin of the back. If they curl when they hit the pan, you're doing it just right. I've eaten everything from trout soup to "poached trout with black bean sauce." For my tastes, there is nothing that tops butter-fried brookies with a blast of salt and pepper. Blow off the lemon.

A favorite once a year shopping trip is to a small mountain brook that is loaded with stunted brookies. If the trout gods smile, I'll take a dozen three- to five-inchers. As they fry up, they curl like Cheetos, as their light orange flesh takes on deeper color with the cooking. Although my wife and daughter will fiddle more with them on the plate, I remove only the heads, gill platelets, and as many fins as is convenient, then eat them whole or in a couple of bites.

The absolute freshest fish I ever ate was part of a culinary experiment—*truite au bleu*. Camped out at a mountain lake, a friend and I caught a nice pair. We put them, live, on a "stringer" of 3X tippet and proceeded to build a fire about twenty feet away. While the butter melted in the frying pan, we apologized to the trout for the fatal affront and their last hour of indignity, and then dispatched them by beheading with a sharp knife. They were instantly gutted and run the twenty feet to the waiting pan. Yes, they did acquire that blue hazy hue but, more significantly, they were literally hopping around in the pan during the first few moments of cooking. Although a little spooked, we pronounced them excellent fare.

It is the one and only time that I have put a live trout on a stringer.

Another Bad Idea

Unless you are a fisheries biologist, working toward some higher purpose, pumping the stomach of a trout to "see what they've been taking" is not only disgusting but shows, I think, a profound lack of respect for these most wondrous companions. And, let's face it, you've already found out what they're taking—the very fly that you were just using.

Breaking Off

Fly fishers will mostly mention "breaking off" in terms of a big fish, as in "The sonavabitch made a run for it and broke me off." Despite such widespread reporting, we all know that this is *not* the single most common reason for broken leaders. No one ever includes in their fishing report, "Four of my backcasts got hung up in trees, and I had to break off," or, "I snagged on a nice deepwater chunk of granite, and it broke me off."

In most Vermont stream fishing, the fact is, if you're not losing flies, you're not fishing right. So, I will concede that we all must forfeit a percentage of our lures to the physical obstacles of our setting, especially on the backcast. But there is a certain mystery that has always puzzled me. It occurs when I've risked a fly against getting hung up on bush or limb and lost the bet. There's my fly, snagged fast, along with a couple of feet of leader that threaten to need retying. Not a bit of line or leader has touched the water yet. The fly is imminently retrievable, simply by reeling up and taking the easy wade to grab it hands on. Of course, if I've been doing my job correctly, it is snagged right in the vicinity of some choice piece of water that I had selected for attention. I try every pull and yank trick in the book. The fly holds fast. Faced with the possibility of spooking the hole, nine out of ten times I will break off. Before I do, I will pinpoint the exact location with a dozen different coordinate markers. Most times, I can even see the fly's location exactly and plainly. Now, the mystery is this: Where the hell do those flies go? With the leader still attached, I expend considerable effort to dislodge the fly, only to fail. Once that leader has broken, however, the same fly will disappear into the great ether nine times out of ten, joining, no doubt, millions of unpaired socks from the washers and dryers of America.

How Many Angels Can Dance on the Head of a Pin?

A nagging ethical question arises regarding just when it is justifiable to break off that stray branch or two that gets in the way of making a decent cast into a favored hole or run. Those of the Chainsaw School of thought on these matters are clearly not only overzealous and unsporting but are surely environmentally harmful.

My own modest take on this subject is that I will not *a priori* groom a casting space. If, however, my fly is laid claim to by any and all manner of obstructions, both above and below water, I will, at my discretion, pillage and burn to retrieve it. If the result of the struggle leaves my next cast with a little more room, or allows my wet fly to pass unimpeded, all the better.

Ice-Out

Every fishing soul that I know talks about "hitting ice-out," that relatively short window of time during which the fish go nuts up top. As the ice clears, the trout, which have been locked under ice for months, turn their attentions to the surface. Here the warmer water, early insect activity, and general exuberance of the fish lead to a feeding frenzy.

For me, ice-out is a sort of Brigadoon. I refer here to that Celtic-legend-made-Broadway-musical-made-movie about a marvelous village of dancing people that, along with the lead's love interest, appears only every hundred years or so. My own classic encounter with ice-out was at Little Elmore Pond.

I've never been hit harder or quicker by first-day brookies than at that memorable thaw. The coarsely broken ice kept blowing in and blowing out on me as I cast from shore. There was brilliant sunshine. It would have been enough of heaven just to have that warm wind against my face and hear the crackle, hiss, and tinkle of the floe as it undulated forward and then in retreat from the fickle breeze. The fishing was fabulous. As the ice floe advanced, it closed the water off to casting. As it retreated, however, and opened that dark water to early-April's sunshine, six- to eight-inch brookies were hammering any fly that I threw at them. The celebration lasted all afternoon, and the brookies' only respite from me was when the wind swung around and blew the floe back against me and the shoreline. Biding time for the floe to ebb and open up the water was like waiting to open wrapped packages on your third birthday.

It's been a quarter-century since I chanced on that magical coincidence of geography, elevation, climate, and timing that yields hungry trout from under the ice. Like the lover in Brigadoon, though, I have been smitten. Come spring, I always go in search of the blessed event.

The Last Cast

As important as the first cast is, it is the last cast that is the really consequential one. Upon this cast depend such diverse things as love relationships and job performance evaluations. As long as there is light, there is hope, and I find myself making "one last cast," like a kid trying to leave the basketball court but needing to make that last shot. Even if you do get a fish on, the last cast is the hardest cast of all.